# SINK OR SWIM

## Real-life Stories on the Clearwater

## THE LIFE CENTER

Published in Beaverton, Oregon, by Good Catch Publishing.
www.goodcatchpublishing.com
V1.1

*Printed in the United States of America*

# TABLE OF CONTENTS

# DEDICATION

This book is dedicated to all the people who have navigated the turbulent waters of life and found a new life of peace, healing and happiness. You are our heroes.

It is also dedicated to those who are still paddling through the rough waters. May you find some hope, help and strength in these pages.

# ACKNOWLEDGEMENTS

I would like to thank Pastor Kelly Lineberry for the vision he had from the beginning and the hard work, prayer, faith and the effort he put into making this book come to life; for the people of The Life Center in Kamiah, Idaho, and their boldness and vulnerability in telling the stories that touch our lives in this compilation of real-life stories.

This book would not have been published without the amazing efforts of our project manager, Marla Lindstrom Benroth. Her untiring resolve pushed this project forward and turned it into a stunning victory. Thank you for your great fortitude and diligence. I would also like to thank our invaluable proofreader, Melody Davis, for all the focus and energy she has put into perfecting our words. Lastly, I want to extend our gratitude to Evan Earwicker, our graphic artist, whose talent and vision continually astound us. We are so blessed to have you as a part of this team.

Daren Lindley
President and CEO
Good Catch Publishing

# INTRODUCTION

We have all experienced troubled waters in our lives at one time or another. In *Sink or Swim: Real-life Stories on the Clearwater,* we tell a few stories of people who have navigated the deep, dark, troubled waters in their lives — some have survived Class 5 rapids. They've crashed on the rocks as the muddy torrents of life unmercifully raged against them and gotten stuck in whirlpools and undercurrents that threatened to take them down for the last time, but they are *survivors.* And not just survivors. Today the waters have cleared, the noise of dangerous rapids subsided and they experience the refreshing and life-giving streams of freedom and purpose.

These stories will captivate your imagination and warm your heart.

Every one of these stories is true — about real people in the Upper Clearwater Region. In some cases, names have been changed to protect related parties from embarrassment by being unnecessarily exposed.

Strap on your life jacket, pick up your paddle, jump on the raft and ride the wild currents with us as you open these pages.

# THE COACH
## THE STORY OF ED AND JEAN JACOBY
### WRITTEN BY ANGELA PRUSIA

JEAN:

"I swear I'll do it this time!" Daddy held the gun to his head. His threats poisoned the air.

My sister slept while I stood at the doorway, shaking. I squeezed my eyes shut; I wished the fighting would stop.

"I was just dancing!" Mama laughed, her words slurred from the alcohol.

"With every man in the bar," Daddy shot back. I knew the baby would start crying if he didn't calm down.

"So shoot me for having fun," she sneered. "You're gone all the time, and I'm stuck with the kids."

"Someone's gotta pay the bills."

"So you can have fun, but I can't?" Mama yelled.

"I'm working. I can't help the hours."

"I'm not stupid." Bitterness laced Mama's words. "What's her name?"

"There's no one!" Daddy thundered. "How many times do I have to tell you that?"

Mama snorted.

"You don't believe me?" Daddy cocked the gun. "Then I'll prove it."

❧ ❧ ❧

# SINK OR SWIM

**ED:**

Leaves rustled as I peered through the branches. The orange crate wobbled on its perch when I shifted my weight.

"Ready?" my best friend from next door yelled from the ground below.

Anticipation filled me. I wanted to fly just like the pilots I heard about from my dad who was in the Navy.

"Ten, nine, eight …" the countdown began.

I grabbed the sides of my aircraft.

"… three, two, one." He brought down the ax and sliced the rope that held me in place.

"Yeehaw!" I whooped. For the briefest of moments, I was flying. Just as quickly, gravity took over, and I plummeted to the ground.

*Bang!* The box splintered on contact. *Bam!* My head smacked the ground.

"Ed-deeeeee!" Mom came out wringing her hands on a dish towel. My sister followed three steps behind. "Are you trying to kill yourself?"

I sat up, dazed, but not hurt. "Did you see me? I was flying."

Mom grabbed my shoulders, her eyes full of fear. Apparently my stunt ranked worse than me peeing outside. So far, Mom hadn't been able to break me of that habit.

"I'm sorry," I muttered. At least she didn't care that I hosted a weekly track meet for my friends.

# THE COACH

"Promise me you won't try to fly again." Mom pulled me close. "I want you alive when your father comes home from the war."

འ~འ~འ

JEAN:

Daddy never killed himself, but his actions left a deep wound. Because of my insecurity, I wet the bed and stuttered as a child. Reading out loud at school brought waves of humiliation as I tried to get the words to come out of my mouth. Seeing myself in my first grade class picture filled me with shame. My hair stuck up all over, and I looked sad. I vowed then to take care of my own hair and attire. As soon as I could pick potatoes in junior high, I bought my own clothes.

I never doubted my parents' love, but I knew God wasn't the center of their lives. They took us to Sunday school, but never stayed. I believed the Bible and knew God was with me all the time. At 14, I wanted to get baptized, so my mother decided the entire family would take the necessary classes to get baptized and become members of the Methodist church.

འ~འ~འ

ED:

Jean didn't know it, but she was the primary reason I

attended church. In eighth grade, all I could think about was the pretty seventh grade girl who sat in front of me at Sunday school. Her long brown hair fell in curls down her back. We didn't talk much, but I watched her come and go, wishing I had the guts to say more. Then Jean surprised me by asking me to a Job's Daughters' Dance. I didn't know that I was her second choice; she broke up with her first choice because he only wanted to neck.

👈👈👈

JEAN:

"Students," the principal's voice sounded over the PA system, "there's an emergency. We need you to remain calm as we evacuate the building."

I exchanged a look with my friend in the next row. "Fire drill?" she mouthed.

I shrugged. It was probably nothing. Some prank or something.

The principal continued, "The school will close for the rest of the day."

Whoops of pleasure rang through the halls. I grabbed my books and headed outside with the others, disgusted with the kids who pulled the prank. I had a book report to finish, so I headed home. Later we found out it was a bomb threat, but the principal never discovered the culprits.

👈👈👈

# THE COACH

ED:

Jean didn't find out I was one of the pranksters until a high school reunion much later. She would've never dated me if she really knew the cut-up I was. Jean was an honor student; to me, school was something to be endured. I didn't have a serious bone in my body. The inscription on my senior picture read, "Almost killed by a train of thought running through his mind." I passed geometry because I won an arm wrestling match with my teacher. If it weren't for my dad being a former English teacher and his good relationships with the teachers, I might not have graduated.

"You're *not* going to college, *are you?*" My English teacher cornered me on the stage at graduation.

At 90 pounds, Miss Ethel Rottman instilled fear in me like no other teacher. We had gotten off to a bad start the first day of class when I leaned back in my chair, and she kicked it out from underneath me. I smacked my backside on the linoleum floor. Two things she didn't tolerate: chewing gum and leaning back, and I'd committed both crimes.

"You should join the Marines." Her suggestion sounded more like a command. "Then figure out what you want to do."

Years later, I wanted to visit Miss Rottman with my college diploma, even if she was right about me not being ready for school then. My only real goals had been centered on football or track and field. I wanted to be a coach and an Olympic athlete, but I forgot about that after I took a high school agriculture class to learn welding. I figured I could become a cattle rancher, so I enrolled at Montana State for agriculture.

At the end of the semester, the men's dean called me into the office. He didn't waste time. "You need to leave, Ed."

I hung my head. I'd spent more time drinking and hunting rabbits than studying, so it came as no surprise. *How would I face my parents with the news that I was getting kicked out of college?*

"Go home," the dean said. "College just isn't for you."

Dad helped me get accepted at the University of Idaho for the spring semester, but my academic and athletic endeavors continued to decline. Drinking and turning the dormitory fire hose on unsuspecting individuals interested me more than studying. I finished the semester with a grade point average less than 1.0. Maybe college really wasn't for me, so I got a job at the Firestone Tire and Rubber Company in Idaho Falls where the management told me great things about my future.

❧❧❧

JEAN:

Even though I dated Ed at the time, my focus was my senior year of high school where I took Latin and other college prep courses. I wanted to pursue a medical career so I could help heal people.

I knew Ed wasn't perfect, but he always respected my boundaries. Friends in his class couldn't believe we were dating, but I couldn't understand their concerns. We had a peaceful relationship. I wrote Ed every day; the desire for a calm home and a husband whose job kept him home each night blinded me to the full truth.

"It was kind of an initiation thing," Ed told me one day before he left the University of Idaho.

"They took your clothes and left you out on some mountain in the dark?" I couldn't believe the story he shared.

"I had my shorts." He smiled.

I didn't see the humor. *How could guys be so cruel?* "How'd you get back?"

"I slept in a granary and talked a farmer into a ride home the next morning."

Ed failed to mention that he had provoked a fight and that "the initiation thing" was actually retaliation. Of course, I took his side and got angry at the injustice of the whole situation.

When Ed proposed in June, I wore the ring he'd purchased from his aunt's jewelry store with pride. I decided to enroll in a secretarial school so I could help with the bills. I saw marriage as a team, and I wanted to support my husband who was becoming successful at the tire company.

Soon after our January wedding, the space heater in our apartment overheated.

Smoke set off the fire alarm.

"Do you smell smoke?" Ed jumped out of bed. Flames engulfed the hallway. Ed took his brand new coat and threw it over the heater to pull the cord out of the outlet.

"Don't try to stop it," I yelled over the chaos. "We have to get out." The hallway was the only way out, so we rushed for the stairs.

The fire unnerved me, but I was grateful to escape alive with my new husband.

ॐॐॐ

ED:

"How'd you hurt your back?" the doctor asked. The pain had increased over several months until it became unbearable.

I winced. "Moving big construction tires." Pain shot through me, and I could hardly breathe.

The doctor examined me. The diagnosis wasn't good. I had three ruptured disks.

"Eventually you're going to need surgery." He looked at his notes. "But your days at Firestone are over. No more heavy lifting. I suggest you go back to school."

My heart sank. I'd failed miserably at school; what college would accept me? I'd done well at Firestone. *What would I do now?*

The doctor fitted me in a body cast, which I wore for a month.

# THE COACH

Firestone threw me a going away party, and I came home drunk. When I threw up, Jean cleaned up the mess.

"I'm going to help you tonight," she said, pursing her lips together. "But never again."

"Will you tell my mother?" I asked, still young enough to fear her wrath.

"No, but you're never going to get drunk again."

I promised, though discouragement weighed me down. "What am I going to do now?"

"What do you really want to do?" Jean looked me in the eye.

I hesitated a moment, remembering my earlier dreams. "Coach."

"Then, let's make you a coach." Her unselfishness touched me deeply; she was willing to give up her dreams to partner with me.

Now I needed to convince the head of physical education at the university. Dr. Leon Green's department was regarded as one of the top programs in the nation.

"So what makes you think I want a guy like you in this program?" Dr. Green asked me.

I'd bombed last semester. *How could I convince him this time would be different?*

"I'm probably crazy even considering you," Dr. Green told me. "Don't disappoint me."

I received a scholarship to run and jump for the Idaho track program.

Jean's support and my attitude made the difference at school this time. I made the Dean's list and became the best sprinter and long jumper on the team. My teammates elected me as co-captain. I don't know whose surprise was greater — Dr. Green's or mine.

ఇళ ఇళ ఇళ

JEAN:

Ed came to the attorney's office where I worked. "There's been an accident at the high school. It's your brother."

"I know." I teared up again. "I've been in the back room praying. Mom just called." Shock hit in waves. This couldn't be happening. Jimmie couldn't be dead. He'd graduate from high school in less than a month.

We drove home to Idaho Falls that afternoon. The accident shook the town. My brother had been pinned by a school bus when the brakes failed on a car he and a friend were driving out of the high school's automotive garage.

Tragedy struck again 12 days later. My brother-in-law died when a train hit the grain truck he was driving. My parents were never the same. Soon after, I lost our first baby in a miscarriage.

ఇళ ఇళ ఇళ

ED:

"Ed, you're the only son I have left." My father-in-law's eyes watered. "You know the plans Jimmie and I had to open a road-paving business when he graduated."

I nodded, not sure where the conversation was headed. "I'd like you to become my partner."

Emotions played across my face. I appreciated the honor, but I had other dreams.

"Thank you." I shifted my weight. "It means a lot that you asked, but I really want to coach."

My father-in-law was disappointed, but he stuck out his hand. "Well, if you're going to coach, I expect you to be a very good one — an Olympic coach."

*Yeah, right.* I almost laughed. *Like that's ever gonna happen.*

࿂࿂࿂

JEAN:

"You gotta go check on Mom," my sister Pat called. "I think she's going to kill herself."

"Mom said that?" I asked. The baby cried from her crib.

"Kind of." I could hear the impatience in Pat's voice even across the miles. "Something's not right. She wasn't talking sense on the phone. Can you go?"

"Yeah." I hung up and called out to Jake and Lorrie. "Come get on your shoes. We need to see Grandma."

I helped them since neither could tie their laces and picked up Karla, who was only a few months old. Not long after, we pulled up to my parents' home.

"Mom!" I opened the door and called out, but no one answered. Jake and Lorrie ran in opposite directions.

"Oh, no," I muttered, careful not to alarm the children. Mom sat in the hallway, her back against the wall. A bottle of Dad's prescription medicine lay empty beside her.

"Mom, it's me. Jean." I shifted Karla and bent to rouse my mom, but she wouldn't respond. A cigarette butt lay between her fingers near a black ring on her shirt. She didn't even know she'd burned her stomach.

I grabbed the phone and called the ambulance, which soon arrived. "What's wrong with Grandma?" Jake asked.

"Nothing, honey," my voice trembled. "She just needs to see the doctor."

Satisfied, Jake ran around the room making siren noises while the EMTs loaded my mother onto a stretcher.

Mom stayed a few days at the hospital for observation. The doctors wouldn't release her until she agreed to go home with Dad.

"No," Mom refused. Their marriage had always been rocky, but since the deaths of my brother and brother-in-law, my parents fought constantly.

The doctor pulled me and my sister aside. "She needs mental help. The risk is too great she'll try suicide again."

Reluctantly, we took Mom to the mental hospital in Blackfoot. She stayed there several weeks until she finally agreed to come home to Dad. Their relationship deteriorated further as they buried their grief in alcohol and drugs. My parents finally divorced after 37 years of marriage.

Despite my mother's issues, we stayed close. I'd had to grow up fast, so I didn't have false expectations. At the same time, I struggled constantly over boundary issues with my mother-in-law.

"Here you go, Jake. Come look what I bought for you." My mother-in-law took a brand new coat out of a department bag soon after Jake started first grade. Except for the red color, the coat was identical to the one I'd bought only days earlier.

Familiar anger burned inside me. "Jake has a coat," I reminded her. "It's black." Work and raising kids kept me busy enough. Jake was an active boy; a black coat wouldn't show dirt nearly as much, which saved me another load of laundry.

My mother-in-law brushed over my comment. "The black one's so plain. I like the red better." She helped Jake into the coat. "What do you think of this one, sweetie?"

I held my tongue. We were so poor, if my mother-in-law wanted to buy a new coat, I would've gladly accepted the gift. Ed and I barely made it from month to month, so the money I spent on the first coat could've gone to other needs.

Later, I confronted Ed. "You have to say something to your mom. Jake doesn't need two coats. We could barely afford the one we bought."

"She just wants to spoil her grandkids." Ed crawled into bed beside me. "She's a grandma."

I wanted to scream. The woman needed boundaries even if Ed wanted to honor his parents like the Bible said. *But how could I convince my stubborn husband of that?*

I turned toward the wall, feeling the anger harden inside me. I cried myself to sleep when he said unloving things or took his mother's side and refused to stick up for me, his wife. During these early arguments, his anger boiled over, surprising me. Several times he punched his fist through a wall. Ed only pushed me once, in the butt during my pregnancy with Jake. After my painful childhood, I refused to allow violence in our home, but that didn't stop Ed's hurtful words.

ED:

My coaching career began to soar. After four years at the high school level, I was selected to receive a fellowship to get my master's degree at Northern Colorado for a pilot project in physical education for the handicapped. Amazingly enough, the recommendation that impressed the committee came from my now good friend, Dr. Leon Green; I was one of 13 chosen from around the country. Later, I was able to recommend him to the University of Idaho Hall of Fame.

I finished two more years at Idaho Falls and then accepted a job at College of the Canyons in California as the track and field coach and chairman of physical education. After four years, Boise State University offered me a job, where I began the first year of my 24-year coaching career there.

Shortly after our move, Jean had other news.

"I'm pregnant, Ed."

I clenched my fists. I didn't want another kid. It was 1973, and abortion had just been legalized. "Get rid of it."

Jean's face fell, but I didn't care. I had enough pressure at work. Coaching at the collegiate level came with a whole new level of responsibility.

᠅᠅᠅

JEAN:

In my spirit, I knew the abortion was wrong, but I feared our marriage wouldn't last if I didn't follow through with the procedure. Many coaches at Boise State were on second or third marriages, and affairs were rampant. If I followed through with the pregnancy, Ed would not be happy, and the rest of our family would suffer. I couldn't risk that.

If I could rewind the clock, I would've never walked into that hospital. The physical toll was difficult enough; aborting a baby halts a woman's body in the middle of nurturing the life within. The natural cycle is disrupted, and the brain has to sort through mixed messages. The emotional and spiritual toll is even greater. Guilt is its own private hell.

We hadn't found a Methodist church since we moved to Boise, and I desperately needed a church. I began watching Robert Schuller on television and discovered "Focus on the Family" with James Dobson.

"If you've had an abortion," Dr. Dobson said over the airwaves, "God will forgive you the moment you ask him. I suggest writing your child a letter. This will help you heal."

"Dear Baby," I wrote one day. "I'm so sorry …" My tears stained the crisp paper as I poured out my heart to the child I couldn't see until heaven. I asked God to forgive me, and slowly I learned to forgive myself.

≈≈≈

ED:

I didn't fully grasp my selfishness or appreciate Jean's pain until I became a Christian. I thought I was a Christian; I'd even prayed for years, but going to church doesn't make a person a Christian any more than going to the doctor makes you a doctor.

"Can we try Pastor Ted's church?" Jake asked one day. My son played football for Borah High School, and Ted Buck, who had played for Borah years earlier, prayed with the players before each game.

Walking through the church doorway, I sensed the difference immediately. People openly expressed their love for God — something I'd never seen.

# THE COACH

"Pastor Ted says it's the Holy Spirit," my son explained. "The Spirit takes up residence inside you when you ask Jesus into your heart." He asked me if I wanted to go to the altar, and I agreed.

Walking up to that altar was the most important event in my life. I've received many awards: 11 Big Sky Conference Coach of the Year awards, four NCAA District Coach of the Year awards, induction into three Halls of Fame and the honor of Boise State naming their track after me, but nothing means as much to me as the moment Jesus transformed my life.

My coaching began to change the more I understood faith as a relationship versus a religion. The more I focused on Jesus, the less I worried about my coaching successes and the more aware I became of the individuals I coached. I became less selfish and more compassionate. I saw my awards as opportunities to share accolades with my wife and kids, without whom I wouldn't be honored.

☙☙☙

JEAN:

"We need to talk, Karla." Ed and I confronted our youngest daughter.

"Lorrie told you." She frowned.

I nodded. "She's worried you'll abort the baby."

"That's what everybody keeps saying," Karla opened up. "Even one of the boosters offered to pay for it."

# SINK OR SWIM

The news didn't shock me; not one person had tried to stop me when I faced the same decision.

"And what about you? What do you want to do, Karla?"

She sighed, but didn't cry. Karla was a strong woman; she had to be strong as an athlete with her dad as a coach. "I don't want to quit school. Not with a full-ride scholarship for track. And Chris doesn't want to get married."

"We'll help you," Ed reassured her. "Pay for the medical bills, help with child care, whatever." I knew Ed regretted our abortion as much as me. Over the years, he'd told me he wondered about the baby and how he or she would've grown up. Like me, Ed had asked God for forgiveness once he realized how he grieved the heart of God.

"Just don't abort the baby," I pleaded. "You'll regret that decision for life."

Seven months later, our grandson Jesse arrived, and we all fell in love with him. Karla finished school and eventually married Chris. They have two more precious children, Jenne and Jade.

"Thank you," Karla tells us over and over, and I see her pride. Jesse is now 23, a star basketball player at Fresno Pacific University. God has used Jesse and his siblings in our lives to break down the walls of prejudice.

My seven grandkids are the treasure of my life. I tell each one — Drew, Jesse, Jenne, Jade, Luke, Karlie and Joy — that God made them exactly the way they are for his purpose. All our talents and colors of skin are beautiful to God.

&#x223F;&#x223F;&#x223F;

ED:

"I'm quitting!" I stomped into the kitchen and spewed out my frustration after a conference meet. "I give it my all, and these kids don't give their personal best."

"You can't quit, Dad!" said Lorrie. "You were made to be a coach. And I'm proud of you."

I stopped ranting. I shouldn't have been surprised by my daughter's strong opinion since she's so much like her mother, becoming a registered nurse to help people. I had no right to make this decision without consulting the people it would impact most — my family, the Jacoby team. Not long after, I'm so glad my family helped me stick with coaching.

One day, Cindy Greiner, The Athletics Congress (TAC) champion in the1984 and 1990 heptathlon, and her husband asked me if I would coach Cindy while she trained for the Olympics. I knew how much of a commitment that meant — training almost four hours a day, six days a week for four years on top of my coaching job at Boise State — but again my family encouraged me. Jean sealed the deal. "You should do it, Ed. You're a great coach."

Then, John Chaplin, a friend I'd run against at

# SINK OR SWIM

Washington State, asked me if I wanted to help with TAC, The Athletic Congress (which became the USA Track and Field, USATF, in 1992). The Olympic Development Committee was a subcommittee of TAC, so I knew the offer meant a lot of work, but I wanted to get involved. During the annual convention, I was selected to become an assistant coach for the 1992 Olympic Games in Barcelona, Spain.

I couldn't believe the opportunity to coach some of the best athletes in the world. *Me? A small-town kid, a goof-off no one thought would graduate?* My father-in-law's words replayed in my mind. *If you're going to coach, I expect you to be a very good one — an Olympic coach.* If only he could've lived to share the moment.

I worked with the men's high jumpers, pole vaulters and discus throwers. The level of competition was so tense and the expectations so great, I didn't fully appreciate coaching Olympic athletes until much later. In addition, I helped two Bahamians, Troy Kemp and Wendell Lawrence, who were both athletes I'd coached at Boise State. I coached Hollis Conway at the elite high jump program, and he tied Poland and Austria for bronze in the high jump.

"Thanks, Coach." Cindy found me at the end of the heptathlon. She finished ninth with her best score ever. "I couldn't have done it without you."

"Who am I going to argue with now?" I smiled at her. For four years, we butted heads like two bulls. She hadn't gotten to that level of competition without strong will, determination and talent. Our biggest conflicts came when I wanted her to change the way she'd done something for years.

"I'll visit. And there's always the phone." Cindy laughed, and we embraced.

৵৵৵

JEAN:

No one was more surprised than me when Ed walked up to the altar and surrendered his life. Suddenly, all the pain in our marriage made sense. Prior to that, Jesus hadn't transformed Ed's heart. Because Ed went to church, I made assumptions. If I'd known Ed hadn't given his life to Christ, I never would've married him. Now that Ed was a Christian, he was changing, but not always fast enough for me.

*I want out,* I vented to God after another conflict with my mother-in-law during the time Ed coached Cindy.

*If you leave*, God said, *I can't accomplish the purpose I have for your lives.*

I knew then God put us together.

Not long after, God showed me that I didn't love Ed unconditionally. My kids were easy to love without condition, but I had little patience with my husband. Even my kids reminded me, "Dad's not the same, Mom. He's different."

Ed wasn't the only one who needed changing. So did I.

# SINK OR SWIM

A friend invited me to Abundant Life Chapel in Kooskia, so I began attending on Tuesday mornings and Wednesday nights. When Abundant Life Chapel joined with the New Life Chapel in Kamiah to become The Life Center, Ed really connected with Pastor Kelly, so we became members. We both appreciate the mission statement of The Life Center: "Loving God Passionately and Loving Others Purposefully." The church is the people; we have no walls.

I am amazed at how much we've grown over the last five years. God has been using my passion for prayer and ministry to help the sick and brokenhearted. Ed sees his mission to minister to coaches and athletes. God has transformed Ed into a generous and selfless man; he invites everyone to our home and recently led a fellow coach to accept Christ.

ED:

The year after I coached in the Barcelona Olympics, I became the men's head coach for the World Championships in Stuggart, Germany. I watched the 4x100 with more anxiety than ever in my entire coaching career. *What if we lost?* I'd be ripped to shreds.

"What are you thinking?" an agent yelled in my face. "I want my guy in the relay."

Someone in the media fired off more questions. "Carl

# THE COACH

Lewis is the fastest runner in the world. Why wouldn't you choose him?"

I'd learned many years earlier I couldn't please everyone, but sticking to my decisions became challenging. I had formed a close relationship with the Lord, and he was honing my attitudes regarding honesty, integrity and the ability to make decisions and stick with them. Without this, I might have caved in to the pressures. The stakes were high. Most of these athletes stood to gain up to a million dollars if they were selected for a relay and won a gold medal. I wasn't worried about the 4x400. The United States was favored to win, and we did, setting a new world record at 2:54:29. Michael Johnson, a brilliant sprinter, ran the last 400 meters in 42.9 seconds. The crowd went crazy.

It was the 4x100 that ate me up, but I wouldn't waver in my decisions. I didn't have to explain myself to a bunch of reporters. We had standards in qualifying, and I would make substitutions in the quarter rounds as necessary to cut down on injuries. Jon Drummond, Andre Cason, Dennis Mitchell and Leroy Burrell would run in the finals. They tied the world record in the semi-finals; now it all came down to the finals.

I stood on the track, nearly sick to my stomach.

The gun sounded, and Drummond sprinted down the track, taking the lead. The crowd screamed with excitement. He handed off the baton to Cason who kept the lead, albeit small. Great Britain and Canada tried to close the gap. Mitchell grabbed the baton and sprinted toward the anchor man. Leroy Burrell ran hard, crossing the finish line 0.04 of a second behind the world record, but 0.29 seconds ahead of Great Britain. The United States won the gold at 37.48 followed by Great Britain at 37.77 and Canada at 37.83 seconds.

"We did it!" My coaches erupted in jubilation around me.

I wiped the sweat from my brow. "Yes, we did."

Psalm 37:4 reads: "Delight yourself in the Lord and he will give you the desires of your heart." Not only did God allow me the incredible opportunity to coach the Olympics and World Championships, he blessed me again when my son got hired at Boise State.

"I thought you'd like to hear the news." My coaching colleague at Boise State found me on the track. "I hired Jake." He grinned. "If he's anything like his old man, he'll be a great coach."

Memories rolled over me. The day Jake became the first high school athlete in Idaho to jump more than seven feet in the high jump, the day he chose Boise State so I could coach him, the day he became the national NCAA high jump champion, our days on the track together.

"Really?" Tears leaked down my face. I didn't have a farm to leave my kids. Coaching was my legacy, their inheritance from me and Jean. Coaching — and faith.

On my mother's deathbed, she asked me to forgive her for meddling too much in our marriage. The next morning, I saw a brilliant light, as bright as the sun. Mom walked toward me through grass so vivid, I'd never seen

# THE COACH

that shade of green. She looked nearly 50 years younger and wore a white robe and her feet, which once hurt so much, were bare. Mom smiled at me and walked off into the distance. The glimpse both excited and encouraged me.

Jesus is the ultimate coach, though. The maker of the universe runs beside us, guiding us, encouraging us, even butting heads with us when we decide we know best and fall instead. Jesus says in John 15:5: "I am the vine; you are the branches. If a man remains in me and I in him, he will bear much fruit; apart from me you can do nothing." Without God, we run without purpose, hitting dead ends and running in circles. With God, we run with victory, someday to stand before him and be crowned with eternal life.

# THE LONELY ROAD
## THE STORY OF JOHN SWEARINGEN
### WRITTEN BY KAREN KOCZWARA

*That's it. I'm going to end it all.*

My heart raced as I held the Magnum gun just inches from my head. Six fresh bullets lay inside the metal casing, but if all went as planned, I'd only need one. With trembling hands, I cocked the gun. In just seconds, it would be all over. No more pain, no more heartache, no more loneliness.

Above my head, the sun shone brightly, promising another glorious spring morning. On days like this, most people would find some excuse to spend time outdoors in the beautiful Idaho mountains. And, once upon a time, I would have been one of them. But not today. Today was different. Today was the last day of my life.

Taking a deep breath, knowing it would be my last, I pulled the trigger …

❧❧❧

For most little boys, the rural mountains of northern Idaho are the perfect backdrop for an idyllic childhood. The sparkling Clearwater River ran through our small town of Kooskia, beckoning the locals to come explore and fish. Vast mountains dotted with tall pine trees surrounded our town at all angles, ideal for wilderness hiking, hunting and camping. With mild temperatures year round, Kooskia was the picturesque place to spend a summer or winter or live all year long.

Growing up in a small town, it seemed everyone knew everyone. A trip to the local post office, grocery store or church meant running into familiar faces who called out your name with a smile and a wave.

For most, it was safe and comforting, but for me, it was lonely. A shy boy of medium stature, I learned early on that it's sometimes in these familiar places that the hurt can sting the most.

"John, I can't hear you! Speak up!" my first grade teacher barked, peering over her reading book with an unimpressed glare.

"I'm tryin', Teacher," I mumbled, staring hard at my book. The words blurred before me, taunting me as though to say, "We know you can't read us! Don't even try!" My cheeks flushed as I felt the stares of my fellow classmates.

"He can't read nothin'!" a boy behind me called out, snickering. The rest of the class went into a fit of giggles. "He's nothin' but a dummy!"

I opened my mouth to protest, but no words came out. Tears burned my eyes as I hung my head and slowly closed my book. It was no use pretending I could read when everyone knew that I couldn't. I waited for the teacher to defend me, but she didn't. Instead, when I glanced up, her amused smile sent fury through my bones. I wanted desperately to race out of my seat and right out of that schoolhouse right then — but I knew that'd spell deeper trouble.

The oldest of five children, I found myself often lost in the chaos at home. My father, a logger, traveled extensively, sometimes leaving home for two to three weeks at a time. We occasionally spent a weekend hunting or fishing together, but for the most part, my father was absent from my daily life.

My mother, a homemaker, tried her best to juggle her daily duties and attend to five active children while my father was gone. Keeping up with a large countryside property was a full-time job. I longed to be close to both my parents and siblings, but in reality, I felt alone most of the time.

"Mama, I scraped my knee," I hollered from the back porch one morning after falling outside. I bent down to inspect the damage as my mother came to my side.

"Oh, now, that's nothing at all," my mother replied hastily. She returned with a bandage, cleaned me off and bustled back into the kitchen to finish dinner.

I watched after her, half hoping she'd run back and plant a big kiss on my forehead or pull me in for a long hug. But alas, she was busy as usual, and I was simply in the way.

Anger mounted in me as I stood to my feet. Even as a very young child, I'd had a temper; the littlest things could send me into a fit of rage so thick that I wanted to throw punches at the nearest person who stepped my way. Years later, I would come to understand that this anger stemmed from my constant loneliness and desire to be understood and loved.

In elementary school, I joined the 4-H program and enjoyed learning how to raise livestock and cook meals. My 4-H leader was a kindly woman who began picking my brother and me up for church on Sundays. The little church met in a one-room schoolhouse and consisted of only a few dozen members. I was intrigued by this Jesus the pastor talked about from the pulpit and hung on every word as he read out of his thick black Bible. Jesus, the pastor explained, loved the world so much that he came to earth to die for our sins so we might live with him in heaven someday. I wanted to know more, but Jesus was not something we talked about much in our home.

My sixth grade year, a local minister invited us to his house. His daughter and I were acquaintances from school, and our families began spending a good deal of time together. Our family began attending his church on and off, and I came to look forward to Sundays more than any other day of the week. I wanted to know more about this Jesus, the one who could be my friend and my savior.

One week at church, my teacher handed me a small New Testament Bible. "This is yours to keep," she explained kindly. "You can read all about Jesus from this book anytime you want to."

"Thank you!" I clutched the Bible tightly to my chest, excited to have my very own book about Jesus. Perhaps he could help fill the void I felt in my heart and help ease the loneliness that encompassed me day and night.

# THE LONELY ROAD

As I grew older, I spent more time outdoors by myself. Many times after school, I hopped on my horse and took off into the wilderness with my dog by my side, sometimes not coming home until after dark. It was soothing being alone with my animals out in the middle of nowhere, away from the people who seemed to look right past me each day. I often thought about God on these long treks, wondering if he really cared about an average boy like me. I wanted to believe he did, but I wasn't quite sure. My own father had a difficult time showing his love; could a heavenly father really care any more?

When I was 12 years old, my father and I got into a terrible fight. The air grew thick with tension as angry words flew back and forth from our mouths. "You need to just leave, John! Get out of this house right now!" my father yelled, his lips curled into a disgusted snarl.

"Fine! I will!" I stormed up to my room, gathered a few things and tossed them into a backpack. Moments later, I slammed the door and headed down the road, my thumb out. I was angry at my father for never being home, for never understanding me for the person I was. Wasn't a father's oldest son supposed to be his pride and joy? Had I failed him?

Daylight turned to dusk as I trudged along, hitching rides whenever I could. I'd been so angry I'd hardly paid attention to where I was going. The paved road wound before me like a dark snake slinking between the mountains. I knew I should turn around, but I didn't want to go home. In fact, I wanted to go anywhere but home, even if that meant spending the night alone in a strange place.

A large green sign ahead read "Utah." I had gone so far south I'd nearly reached another state! A thrill ran through my spine at the thought of being so far away from home, and I kept on walking. I was just two miles inside the Utah border when a police car approached me alongside the road.

"Your folks have been looking for you, son. Time to go home."

I was half relieved, half angry that my parents had gone looking for me. I'd almost expected them to wave their hands and say, "Oh, well, that John. Better that he's gone now." I sheepishly climbed into the police car, which turned around and took me to the Grangeville police station back home, where my parents were waiting for me.

"What on earth were you thinking, riding off to the Utah border?" my mother cried, pulling me in for a hug.

"I'm sorry I lost my temper with you, son," my father said quietly, clearing his throat. He patted my arm awkwardly. "Please come back home now."

I fought back tears as I went inside the house. I was glad to know my parents had missed me, but the lonely ache inside my chest now burned even greater than before. Would I always feel this way, like an outsider looking in? Would I ever find my place in this world?

High school rolled around, and I threw myself into sports, including track, football and baseball. The rugged Idaho wilderness was my playground on the weekends. I hunted, fished and camped during the summers and kicked up the snow with my snowmobile when winter rolled around. As busy as I was, I still had very few close friends. My freshman year, I met a boy named Forrest who was two years my junior; he became my closest friend. He encouraged me to go back to church and seek after God.

I began attending church again and was intrigued as the pastor read from the Bible. Memories of the small church I'd attended with my 4-H leader popped into my mind. I had been so eager back then to learn about Jesus and follow him; receiving my New Testament Bible had been almost as exciting as Christmas morning. But over the years, I'd begun to wonder: *Did God really care about the details of my everyday life?* Though I spoke to God on and off, the sad longing in my heart followed me wherever I went.

My junior year, I began dating the girl whose father had invited us to his church. We had been casual friends over the years, but I'd never really thought of her as more than that until now. Suddenly, it seemed she had blossomed into a beautiful woman overnight.

We began to date. My girlfriend's father accepted another pastorate and she moved away, but we continued our relationship long distance. Eventually, I asked her to marry me. She accepted, and we began planning for our wedding. I was thrilled at the idea of finally having a companion by my side for good. Surely, the loneliness would disappear once I said "I do." I would be a good husband, attentive and loving, making sure she knew she was number one in my life at all times.

Two weeks before the big day, I received a phone call from my fiancée's father.

"John, I don't quite know how to tell you this, but she's decided to … to marry someone else. In fact, they've gone off and eloped. I'm so very sorry."

I stared at the phone, his words playing in my head in slow motion. *Someone else. So very sorry.* My head began to spin as I hung up, tears spilling down my cheeks. Surely this couldn't be happening. Surely this was a nightmare. How could she have done such a thing to me, throwing away all we had to run off with some other guy?

A deep loneliness of a new kind settled into my soul as I sank to the floor and began to sob. I'd come so close to finding love, to being able to put my heart on the line, only to have it trampled on once again. It just wasn't fair, it just wasn't right!

On impulse, I gathered a few belongings, grabbed a handful of things to eat and threw them into my horse's saddlebags. Included in these things was a .357 Magnum handgun. I tried not to think too much about the gun and what I might do with it as I rode off into the wilderness, my heart breaking into pieces as the dust swirled behind me.

It was a beautiful spring Idaho day, but I could not appreciate the budding leaves on the trees nor the bits of snow that sat like dollops of white frosting on the mountains ahead. All I could focus on was my mounting loneliness and heartache that seemed to follow me wherever I went. Perhaps if I rode far enough away, it would finally leave me alone; perhaps the heartache would disappear.

I rode a good 13 miles into the wilderness, at last settling on a nice quiet spot beneath a few trees. I stripped the gear off my horse and plopped to the ground, burying my face in my hands as the tears fell. It was too much to bear; I could not go on like this. At last, I looked up to the heavens and shouted, "Okay, God, if you care, make yourself real to me right now, or I'm done!"

I sucked in my breath and waited, half hoping and expecting God to part the heavens and speak to me from above. But nothing happened. I heard only the sounds of a bird chirping. I pulled my knees to my chest and kept waiting, my heart thudding with each passing minute. *Come on, God. Show up! Where are you?*

When two hours passed and still I hadn't heard from God, I pulled the gun from my bag and loaded it with six fresh bullets. My fingers shook with each one I slid in. "You had your chance, God, and you didn't show," I muttered under my breath. "Now I'm really done."

Taking one last deep breath, I cocked the gun, held it to my head and pulled the trigger. My chest tightened as I waited for the loud bang, but to my amazement, nothing happened. Baffled, I pulled the trigger again, and then again, until all six bullets should have been used. Nothing happened!

I dropped the gun on the ground and began to bawl.

# SINK OR SWIM

Thick salty tears poured down my cheeks as I rocked back and forth, amazed at what had just taken place. God *had* shown up. He had heard my cries, and he had stopped that gun from going off. He really did care after all.

I bawled until it felt as if all my tears had been used up. Suddenly, I patted my coat pocket and felt something inside. Curious, I reached in and pulled out my New Testament Bible, the one my Sunday school teacher had given me in the fifth grade. I had no idea how it had gotten in there; its appearance was just as mysterious as the gun failing to shoot. I never carried my Bible in my coat pocket. It was as if God himself had reached down and placed it in there when I wasn't looking.

Too overjoyed to speak, I opened the Bible and began to read, the words filling my soul like good medicine. I began to speak to God, praising him for the miracle I'd just witnessed, for him sparing my life when I'd come so close to ending it all. At that moment, I knew that he did truly care for me and had a plan and a purpose for my life, even though I could not yet see it. And I knew that somehow, no matter what the future held, I was going to be okay.

I stayed in the wilderness for the next couple days, praying, reading my Bible and soaking in the amazing miracle I'd just encountered. My heart felt lighter than it had in years; the loneliness I'd carried around with me like a bag of bricks all my life didn't feel nearly so heavy anymore. I glanced out over the mountains at the beautiful terrain before me, finally taking in the beauty that I'd so often overlooked in the midst of my pain. I was in God's country, and I'd never felt closer to him than I did at that moment.

The morning I decided to leave, I pulled out my gun and tried to fire it to see if it worked. To my amazement, it fired just fine. I fired again, and again, until all six bullets had been used up. Indeed, there was not a thing wrong with the gun or the bullets. There was no explanation other than God had intervened at my darkest moment, saving my life when I'd come so close to ending it all. I praised him the whole way down the mountain.

"You really should get back to church, man," Forrest encouraged me. He had been a constant friend over the years, and I was grateful for his loyalty. Forrest had constantly talked to me about having a deeper relationship with God, and now I was finally ready to take that next step.

With a newfound lease on life, I went to work at a local lumber mill and began to pray about what God might have for my future. Nearly a year later, I met a wonderful girl named Karen through a friend at church. We began dating shortly after. I enjoyed Karen's company immensely but kept my heart on a short leash. The hurt and pain from my previous relationship was still very raw, and I wasn't quite sure I was ready to fully give myself to someone again. To complicate matters, Karen was a minister's daughter. I feared she might leave me just as my ex-fiancée had and wasn't confident my heart could handle another painful goodbye.

# SINK OR SWIM

Karen went to college, and we continued to stay close and write letters. Then one day, she announced she needed to take a break from our relationship. "I need to do this, John. I want to make sure you are really the man for me," she told me quietly.

I was devastated, of course, but tried to remain understanding. If Karen and I were meant to be together in the end, things would work out. I threw myself into my work and outdoor activities but decided to once again take a break from church. All my old insecurities came rushing back as I thought about my future. I'd always equated God's love with man's love; if man let me down, maybe God would as well. Despite the miracle I'd encountered on the mountain, I suddenly felt unsure about my relationship with God once again.

One afternoon after work, I headed home on my motorcycle with my friend by my side. The beautiful warm weather had beckoned to me that morning to ride my bike again. Just outside of Kooskia near the lumber mill, a car ran a stop sign out of the blue. I could do nothing to avoid the car except try to stop. Unfortunately, I hit the brakes just a moment too late. Like a scene out of a suspense movie, I flew up in the air, tumbled over the windshield and landed on the other side of the road in a ditch.

My body ached from head to toe as I lay there, reeling from the pain and the surreal horror that I'd just endured. My head spun as I tried to process what had just happened. Slowly, I pulled myself up off the dirt and put a shaky hand to my head. My helmet was cracked badly, but thankfully, it had served its purpose. My knee and wrist throbbed, but at this point, I was just thankful to be alive. God had spared my life once before, and now he had spared it again. I could live with a few broken bones so long as I could live to see tomorrow.

"You're in pretty bad shape," the doctor at the hospital explained to me as he inspected my injuries. My left wrist was in traction with pins inserted through my wrist all the way up to my elbow. My right leg was in a cast all the way up to my hip. Amazingly, I hadn't sustained any serious internal injuries.

"You lost your knee cap in the accident," the doctor continued. "If we operate, there's only a 50 percent chance that your body will accept a new knee cap. How do you feel about that?"

"Let's leave the knee cap alone," I suggested, trying to smile through my pain. The idea of more surgery didn't sound fun. I'd take a risk and hope that God would heal my bad knee over time.

The doctor shrugged. "All right, it's your call."

Karen came to the hospital when she heard about the accident. Her eyes were filled with concern and compassion as she came to my side. "I'm so glad you're okay, John. I was so worried when I heard the news." She took my hands in hers. "John, I know I said I wanted to take some time apart, but I want you to know that I love you, and I only want to be with you."

Her words were the best medicine any man could have

received. My heart filled with joy as she looked into my eyes, her sweet smile filling the room. I knew without a doubt this was the girl I wanted to marry and spend the rest of my life with.

Shortly after the accident, I asked Karen to marry me, and she happily accepted. As thrilled as I was to be engaged again, a tiny part of my heart still remained cautious as I recalled the events of the past. I knew Karen wasn't going anywhere, but I wasn't sure I could go through such heartache again if she did leave.

I had just gotten my cast off and begun to recover from the accident when another drastic incident occurred. One afternoon, my friends asked if I'd go out and help them fetch some firewood. I threw on a t-shirt as I headed out the door, grateful for another beautiful sunny day.

"Thanks for your help, John," my buddy called out as we lugged the firewood over to be cut.

"No problem," I replied. My arm was still tender from the accident, and my strength was not at its fullest. I thrust the saw into a log and began to saw when suddenly, the saw pinched in the log. I yanked it out and started to go under the log to undercut it when the tip of the bar touched a small limb. The saw kicked back and aimed straight for my neck. In a panic, I threw my arm up to protect myself. Like a vicious animal, the saw attacked my arm before I could pull it away. Instant pain seared through every nerve in my arm as I tried to stay calm.

"Man, help me!" I called out to my friend Larry, grabbing my throbbing arm.

# THE LONELY ROAD

Larry raced to my side, ripped off his shirt and quickly wrapped it around my arm to stop the bleeding. "This looks bad, man. We gotta get you to the hospital quick," he said gravely.

Flashbacks of the motorcycle accident not long ago jogged through my mind as the nurses wheeled me into the emergency room. God had been so good to spare my life during what could have easily been a fatal accident. Though my current injuries were not life threatening, they were quite serious, and I was grateful that I hadn't lost my entire arm in this accident.

"The cut was very deep," the doctors told me as I lay in the recovery room a few hours later. "It took us nearly an hour to sew you back up, son — 357 stitches inside and out, to be exact. But there's no infection, and you're expected to make a full recovery. I suggest you stay out of trouble for a while, if you can."

I let out a small laugh, glancing down at my injuries. Indeed, I was like a cat with nine lives; in my case, I had only six more to spare. If I wanted to make it to my wedding day, I knew I'd better stay in bed for the next few months and avoid any possible catastrophe.

As I spent the next few weeks recovering, I began to reflect on my life over the past couple years since God had protected me from committing suicide. I had been so excited to follow him after riding down that mountain, filled with a hope I hadn't felt in years. Yet since that time, I had found myself in and out of church as a sometimes follower of Christ. I wasn't doing anything particularly "bad," but I wasn't exactly living every day for the Lord, the one who had breathed life back into my tired and wounded soul. In truth, I was still sometimes doubtful of his love. But it was in these dark, scary and uncertain moments that God gently reminded me that his love for me remained the same. He had watched over me numerous times, sparing me from death and tragedy, and I had to believe that, despite my insecurities, he had some greater purpose for my life. Though still a little wary, I was finally ready to give him my all, to follow him with my whole heart. Starting now.

December 28, 1974 was an unforgettable day. Karen and I were married in a beautiful ceremony, and we made our home in Kamiah, Idaho. We talked about having children early on, but I was afraid to have our first child.

"I want it to be a boy," I insisted to Karen one night as we discussed baby plans. "If God gives me a boy, I will know that he truly loves me." It meant so much to me to have my firstborn be a boy; perhaps I hoped that I'd be given a chance to be the kind of father mine hadn't been able to be to me.

Not long after this talk, Karen announced she was pregnant. I was excited and terrified at the same time. I prayed our child would be a boy. Shortly after learning the news, however, Karen lost the baby. We were both devastated. Why would God give us a child only to take it away?

Karen remained positive, however, that we would soon get pregnant again. At last, nearly four years after we married, we brought our first son, Marc, into the world. He was more beautiful than anything I could have imagined, and I marveled at his tiny features for hours, thanking God for such a wonderful gift. Shortly after his birth, however, the doctors realized something was wrong.

"It looks like his lungs are filled with amniotic fluid," one of the doctors said in a concerned tone, whisking him away for further observation. "He's going to have trouble breathing on his own until the fluid dissolves."

Momentary panic rose in my chest. Our beautiful boy, the promise God had given me, a firstborn son, now fighting for his life! I tried to stay strong as I held a weary Karen, assuring her things would be all right. "He'll be okay, I just know it," I whispered softly.

After rushing him to a larger hospital with a neonatal unit, the doctors gave him the care he needed, and within a few days, our son was home with us, snuggled in Karen's arms as he slept contentedly. I marveled once again over this little boy God had given us, thanking God for healing him and promising to be the best father I could possibly be.

Our little boy proved to be a joy in our lives. I kept up my job at a local lumber mill as a lumber grader and spent my free time with my wife and new son. Each time I looked into his eyes, I was reminded of God's goodness and faithfulness to me over the years. And each time I held his little hand, I was reminded of the enormous responsibility God had placed in my hands, to teach my son about Jesus and show his love through my own life.

# SINK OR SWIM

In 1981, our second son was born, and our joy doubled. Three and a half years later, another brother joined our family. We were now bursting at the seams with boy energy and loving every minute of it. Karen scrambled to keep up with three active sons while I worked hard to support our family.

I also praised God for healing my knee. After my motorcycle accident, I'd feared I wouldn't be able to keep up with the outdoor activities I loved, but I was now able to run and jump with my boys just like I'd done as a child.

Indeed, life was good.

And then, in 1991, I got a phone call that rattled me to the core. My younger brother had drowned while floating the Selway River in Idaho on July 6th. Though I had not been especially close to my siblings over the years, I was deeply saddened nonetheless by this loss. I was also reminded of the strained relationship between my father and me over the years. Would I ever be able to talk openly with my father and let him know how he'd hurt me? And would he ever share his heart with me?

Karen and I busied ourselves in our little church in Kamiah, enjoying the various responsibilities we took on in the congregation. Though loneliness still plagued me from time to time, I slowly learned to be comfortable in my own skin. I also learned to control my anger and temper, leaning on the Lord for his strength every day. Having a family of my own had made me feel fulfilled in ways I never thought possible. But having a real and meaningful relationship with Jesus had proven to be even more exciting. Reading my Bible and praying on a daily basis helped remind me that even when I felt completely alone, I never was, because he was always by my side.

A few years after my brother passed away, we received another devastating phone call. My father had suffered a heart attack. Thankfully, God had spared his life and gave him a second chance, like with me. Through this crisis, my father realized that he needed to make things right with God once and for all.

"I want to be a new man, John," my father told me during one of our visits, his voice weak and tired. "I've given my life back over to the Lord. And I want to tell you how sorry I am for the way things were for you growing up. I realize now that you probably never felt very loved by me, and I'm very sorry for that. I did love you but didn't do a very good job of showing it. I never meant for things to be the way they were. Will you forgive me?"

As I looked into his eyes, creased with age and a hard life, it occurred to me that my time with my father on earth could be very short. I didn't want to let the moments pass me by, nursing my hurts from the past and being angry at my father for not showing me his love. I had received the greatest gift of all in my heavenly father's love and forgiveness of my sins; how much easier should it be to accept my earthly father's forgiveness?

"I forgive you, Dad," I told him softly, fighting back tears. "And I love you."As soon as the words escaped my lips, I knew our relationship would never again be the same.

# SINK OR SWIM

My father and I spent the next several years enjoying one another's company. As he lived only three miles from our home, I visited him often, taking him hunting and fishing as we had done when I was a child. We trekked through God's beautiful creation together while catching up on life's adventures over the years. For the first time in my life, I felt free to be myself around my father. And free to accept his love. It was like starting all over again and getting a second chance at the childhood memories we'd been too busy to make years before. Slowly, as I had with Karen, I began to loosen the leash on my heart as my dad and I grew closer.

Then one day, there was more bad news. "I have cancer, John," my father told me gravely. "It doesn't look good."

I was too stunned to speak. Just when my father and I had begun to build a solid, heartfelt relationship, God was taking him from me! Heartbroken, I soaked in the news and prayed for a miracle.

Time passed, and my father's health continued to decline. My heart grew sad as I watched him struggle more to do the daily things he enjoyed. One day, we took a ride out into the wilderness to hunt. As we drove, my father spoke up, sadness welling in his eyes. "John, this is probably going to be the last time I'm going to be able to go hunting with you," he told me quietly.

I nodded my head and gulped. I had known this day was coming but hadn't prepared myself for such heartache. We enjoyed our typical morning of hunting and then spent the remainder of the day driving around, talking about life and saying all the important things we had to say. I was thrilled Dad had a true relationship with God now and would be going to heaven when he died, but I couldn't help but want him on this earth a little bit longer.

In 2000, after two years of battling cancer, my father ingested fluid in his lungs and died of congestive heart failure. I was briefly angry with God for taking away my father at the peak of our relationship. We had just begun to get to know each other, and now, just like that, he was gone. The loneliness I'd struggled with so much of my life resurfaced, and I withdrew a bit from life to grieve alone.

Thankfully, Karen, my boys and her parents remained my rock during this difficult time. Her parents had become like second parents to me, and I highly valued my relationship with them. My mother, who suffered from dementia, grieved in her own way. I clung to the Bible verse Philippians 4:13: "I can do all things through Christ who strengthens me." This verse had served as a constant reminder in my life that, no matter how painful things seemed or how hard life became, God would hold me up, giving me the strength to endure. I knew this time would be no exception.

My mother came to live with our family for a while until she suffered a stroke and it was necessary to move her into a home. Though her mind is not what it once was, she is now able to tell me she loves me, and I believe her from the bottom of my heart. I know now that my mother, like my father, always loved me but just had a difficult time showing it when we were young.

Karen and I are now actively involved in The Life Center Church of Kamiah, Idaho. We feel like we'd rather be nowhere else on earth on a Sunday morning, surrounded by a group of fellow believers who have become our friends and family. The lively Bible-centered services are refreshing to my soul. I currently lead a men's group at the church, something that constantly requires me getting out of my comfort zone as I reach out to other men and encourage them in their relationship with Christ. I feel like I'm home at last.

೩೩೩

As I hop in my car and head off to work at the lumber mill, I thank God for how much he has blessed me with over the years. A wonderful wife, three amazing boys and now three darling grandchildren added to the mix. A church we love, a job I enjoy, a place to call home. It is above and beyond what I could have dreamed up in my wildest imagination.

I meet with my good friend Forrest at work, like I do every morning, and we pray together.

While I grade the lumber, I watch the warm morning sun poke its way through the trees, and my mind drifts back to that lonely little boy of my youth. How I'd longed to be loved and accepted, to be understood. I'd thought for sure that loneliness might haunt me for the rest of my life.

# THE LONELY ROAD

I'd been so hurt, I'd chosen to take my own life on that quiet spring morning years ago. But thankfully, God had spared my life through what could be described as no less than a miracle. To think I might not be here today with all that he's given me … well, it is too hard to fathom. Truly, he is good. And though it took me many years to finally grasp it, I now know God's love is the real deal.

Driving home, just ahead the stunning Idaho mountains come into view, the last of the snow still melting off. Awe overwhelms me as I take in the beauty of it all. The wilderness can be a lonely place, but as I've discovered, it doesn't have to be. For sometimes, it's on that quiet rural road that you realize you aren't traveling alone, but alongside the creator of it all.

# TWO HEARTS
## THE STORY OF KATE AND PATRICK
### WRITTEN BY KAREN KOCZWARA

*Drew is gone.*

I squinted in the bright sunlight as the church doors closed before me. There I stood, alone on the steps, trying to process the devastating news. *Gone. Dead. Not coming back. A drowning accident,* they said. I knew nothing more.

I tried to remember. Had we kissed goodbye before he walked out the door? Surely we had; we were in love. Had I told him I loved him? I hoped so.

A car whizzed by, and I cringed inside. Probably someone out for a nice leisurely drive, blasting their radio and humming along while the breeze whipped at their cheeks, sipping their coffee without a care in the world. Someone whose husband had not just died.

Slowly, I descended the steps and walked toward my car, putting one bare foot in front of the other on the old rough cement; there'd been no time for shoes. The tears would come, I was sure of that. But for now, I had to move forward. Have a plan of action. Later, I could bury my head in my pillow and cry myself dry.

Half an hour ago, I hadn't been a widow. Now, just like that, I was.

Widows were old ladies who wore bunched up nylons

and twisted their hair into buns and sat quietly in the back pew of the church on Sunday mornings. Widows dressed in black and paraded around with pencil-thin frowns and grew sad wrinkles after their husbands died. Would I be like them? Surely, I was too young. There must be some other title for girls like me who hadn't even had a chance to pick out a baby name or paint a nursery yellow with the one they loved.

My life had changed in an instant. I reached for my cell phone and numbly made call after call as I tried to arrange things. As I waited for my parents to show up, I clutched my heart, as though to say, "Not yet. You can break later. We have work to do."

Little did I know, just a few miles down the road, someone else's heart was breaking. Someone with a story of his own, a story that would one day be entwined with mine.

ﻪﻪﻪ

Some people like to plan, while others like to let life guide the way and figure things out as they go. I'm in the former category. I like to have a plan, to know what's next, to map things out with precision and move forward. But sometimes life takes a twist, a turn, and there we are, pencil behind our ear and not a clue what to do next. That is what happened to me.

Growing up in the small town of Kamiah, Idaho, the plan seemed pretty straightforward. My father, a pastor of a small church, was a devoted family man. My mother worked hard at the credit union in town and poured everything she had into my younger sister and me. Though we were poor, our home brimmed with love, life and laughter. I was active in my father's church, singing in the choir and helping out in Sunday school. For the most part, life was good.

Kamiah is a small logging town in northern Idaho, nestled between mountains, rivers and more greenery than I believe God put on most of this earth. The breathtaking Clearwater River runs parallel to the town, living up to its name with deep crystal-clear pools of blue. Locals can take advantage of hunting, fishing, hiking, biking and camping year round, thanks to Kamiah's mild, inviting weather. Many kids often make trouble in small towns, but to me, Kamiah was a little girl's paradise.

School came easily to me from the time I was a young child. I enjoyed every subject on the planet and brought home straight A's. When high school hit, I made the varsity volleyball team. If things went as planned (and I was sure they would), I would nab a full-ride scholarship to Eastern Washington University when I graduated and study to become a high school math teacher.

Halfway through my sophomore year, I started dating a guy named Drew. His parents were in the ministry, too, and we found we had oodles in common. Drew wanted to pursue a career in teaching as well, focusing on high school social studies. Though were six hours apart during our dating relationship, we started discussing the option of future marriage during our junior year. I had no reservations about marrying young; I was ready to start a life with Drew and have a family of our own. Husband? Check. Career plans? Check. Things were moving along.

After Drew and I married, I attended Eastern Washington University for one year. We then moved to Milton-Freewater, Oregon, where his parents pastored a local church. I had always assumed I'd remain active in the church and was excited to see how I could serve in our new congregation. Eager to dive in, I tried to help, but to my disappointment, Drew's parents discouraged my involvement.

Eventually, the church leadership allowed me to serve as a backup singer on the worship team. Drew's parents occasionally paid a visit to our home, during which they pointed out my shortcomings and faults using Bible verses to back up their views. I was hurt and bewildered by their behavior.

Disappointment mounted in me as I continued to be turned down for ministry opportunities in the church. My entire life had revolved around being active in the church. It had never occurred to me that I wouldn't be allowed to make this a full part of my life. Church ministry was a part of who I was. Telling me I couldn't be involved was like ripping off my left arm. Drew's parents' continuous remarks about my spiritual "shortcomings" were like salt in the wound.

"I just don't understand," I lamented to Drew one night. "Why do they feel this way?"

# TWO HEARTS

Drew shrugged. "I dunno. It frustrates me, too. But what can we do?"

*We can protest!* I wanted to shout. But I knew better. Drew had a great deal of respect for his parents, and I needed to let things be. I would throw myself into my job and my role as a new wife. "God, help me to let go of this situation," I prayed that night as I climbed into bed. "I just need to give this over to you."

One afternoon, while driving home from a friend's wedding, I felt God say to me out of the blue, *Kate, you could fail.* Tears pricked my eyes and spilled down my cheeks as I stared out the window. Up until this moment, failure had never been an option for me. Things in life had always come easily; it had never occurred to me that there might come a time when the plan might be detoured. But for the first time, I realized it might. It was a humbling thought.

Eventually, Drew's parents allowed me to become a bit more involved in the worship team at the church, and we became assistant youth leaders. I enjoyed using my gifts again in the church, but it was difficult to put my whole heart into it at times as I sensed their disapproval. By now, nearly two years had passed since we'd moved to Oregon, and I wondered if this cycle of frustration was truly how things were meant to be for Drew and me.

"Where do you see us down the road?" Drew asked me out of the blue one day. "Is this really the life we want and God wants? Maybe we're better off somewhere else." This wasn't the first time we'd had this conversation. The awkwardness between Drew's parents and us had put quite a strain on our new marriage. I wondered if we'd be better off on our own somewhere, making a life for ourselves without the influence of his family. We both agreed that in God's timing we would start seeking a new direction.

"God will open and close doors in his timing," Drew encouraged, putting a hand on my shoulder. "I've got the youth camp coming up, and I need to put all my efforts into that. The kids are really looking forward to it."

Drew knew the weeklong camp in the Washington mountains was going to be difficult in many ways, but he was also eagerly anticipating making a difference in the kids' lives. I knew I needed to be a good support to Drew and pray for him as he ventured out.

The big day arrived, and I helped Drew pack his suitcase, throwing in several warm pairs of clothes and a swimsuit as well. The weather could be quite unpredictable in the Washington mountains, and it couldn't hurt to be too prepared. "I'll miss you," I sighed as we shut the bulging suitcase. "Call me when you get there."

"I will," Drew promised, pulling me close. "I love you. I wish you could come with me."

I'd just started a new job at the bank and couldn't take the time off. I hoped my work would keep me busy so I didn't have to focus on missing Drew. "Be safe," I whispered, planting a kiss on his cheek.

Had I known what was coming next, I would have

held him longer. I would have breathed in his freshly showered scent. I would have stared harder at his every feature, taking in his every gesture and step. But there was no way I could have known when he walked out that door that he might never walk back in again.

Two days later, I was pulling on my jeans after a day at work when the telephone rang. It was Drew's mother; her voice was short and to the point. "You need to come down to the church right now, Kate."

I rushed out the door without slipping on my shoes and drove on autopilot. Her voice had bordered on urgent, but I didn't want to be presumptuous. Maybe it was nothing. Maybe I was going to get reprimanded for something I had done in the church, as I had many times before. Or maybe it was something serious … maybe it was Drew! *No, God, let it not be Drew.*

The sun shone brightly as I pulled up at the little church and walked with lead feet toward the building. I barely felt the old rough concrete on my bare feet, barely noticed the chilly breeze that kicked up out of nowhere and stung my cheeks. I ascended the steps as the big doors swung open and Drew's parents appeared at the front.

"Drew has died," my father-in-law said with a twisted look on his face that I'd never seen before. "He drowned."

"Are you serious — 'cause if you are kidding, this isn't funny," I choked out. They just shook their heads. And then, in a shocking move, my in-laws walked back inside and closed the doors behind them, leaving me standing alone on the step to grieve and process. I watched the doors swing shut, shaking my head in disbelief. *What about me?* I wanted to call after them. *I'm still here! His wife, the widow, standing on the steps alone!*

I'd watched enough movies and TV shows growing up to see people react when someone died. There were all the clichés, of course. Wailing on the ground, shaking their fist in the air in denial, screaming, yelling, moaning, sobbing. I did none of that. Instead, like a robot, I descended the steps and made my way back to the car, my mind instantly racing to what needed to be done next. Ever the planner, I was ready to take action. The crying, the grieving, would come later.

I called my parents first. "Drew's dead," I told them softly, my voice almost breaking. "We need to get to the camp."

Next, I called the youth camp, willing my voice to keep steady as I spoke. "Yes, this is Kate. Drew drowned?" The last part came out as a squeak, a question mark hanging in the air like the rest of my future. "I need to speak to someone who knows what happened."

The local sheriff came onto the line. "I'm so sorry for your loss, Miss. It appears it was a drowning accident. We're still investigating."

Investigating. Yes. That made sense. Trying to put the pieces together, like a puzzle. Suddenly, I sprang to my feet. I needed to get up to that camp right this minute and find out what happened! I needed to put my own pieces together before I fell apart.

My parents picked me up, and we drove through the

night to the camp. No one said much along the ride; what was there to say? I'm sorry? We were all sorry. We were all in shock. But that wasn't going to make us get there any faster, wasn't going to make Drew come home again. I sank into the back seat, gripping the door handle as the car sped along the freeway toward the Washington mountains. My heart beat steadily in my chest, *thump, thump*, just like it should. I expected it to race out of control, but it didn't. It kept beating, for Drew, unwilling to break just yet.

*Maybe it was all a mistake*, I reasoned as we neared the camp. Maybe it wasn't Drew who had drowned, but someone else. But in my gut, I knew better. Drew had never been a great swimmer. A few summers before, the two of us had gone swimming in the Clearwater River. Drew had stuck his feet in gingerly, afraid to go much deeper than his waist. An avid swimmer, I dove right in, teasing him for being so cautious. Drew decided to try and swim across with me and my sister, which ended in the two of us pulling him off the bottom of the river. He was shaking, visibly rattled by the incident. I assured him we would never try that again and never bugged him again about staying where he could securely touch bottom.

When we finally arrived at the camp, I was tired, hungry and in a daze. I stumbled out of the car and made my way toward the chaos. The local cops had been called, and some of Drew's relatives were running to and fro, yelling and screaming and trying to find someone to blame.

# SINK OR SWIM

"You killed Drew!" some of his family wailed, their eyes full of rage as they lunged toward the camp director.

Speechless, the camp director took a step backward, looking both fearful and sympathetic. He had known and loved Drew, and his own grief was written all over his face.

I took it all in like a moviegoer in the third row of the theater, minus the popcorn. And with false reassurance that the drama would all be over in an hour when the credits rolled. Suddenly, I needed to find a quiet, secluded place. I could not breathe; despite the open mountain air, I was suffocating.

I stepped away from the crowd and found my own little place of quiet. For the first time since hearing the news, the tears threatened to come. "God, I need you to be near, right now," I prayed, a sudden ache ripping through my soul. "I need to put my full faith in you, for you are all I have."

As Drew's mom continued to wail in the background, I stayed in my own private world of grief, soaking in God's presence and the quiet of his love. I had a long road ahead of me, but at that moment, I knew he would carry me through.

The next few days were a blur as I went through the motions and tried to understand what had taken place. The story seemed to go something like this: Drew was waiting by himself as a new group of kids were being brought down to the swimming hole. His hat and shoes were found on top of a rock near a waterfall when the kids got there. The kids thought it was one of Drew's infamous

practical jokes. But when he failed to appear after some time, the kids realized it was no joke. Drew's body was found later at the bottom of the waterfall. The cops called it a drowning, a terrible accident. I called it ripping out a piece of my heart.

"Look, this newspaper reports that he was a lifeguard," my mother said quietly, holding up a local newspaper one morning. She shook her head, frustrated, as she read on.

"They got it all wrong! Drew hated to swim!" I grew quiet, thinking about Drew sitting up on top of that rock. The papers could say what they wanted, have their own hunches, but I knew Drew better than all of them. Drew had sat on top of that very waterfall with his friend Timmy in summers past. My two cents said Drew had been sitting up there, reflecting as he had with Timmy, when he had slipped and fallen to his death. But it was no use fighting newspapers when I had a funeral to plan.

The next day, my dad drove me to Vancouver, Washington, to identify Drew's body. I tried to prepare myself for that moment during the dreaded drive to the morgue. *Would it look like Drew, or would he be a stranger? Would I even be able to glance at his body, or would it be too much to bear?*

Drew's parents, little brother and pregnant sister met us at the morgue. The mortician motioned me to come back, and I did. I only needed one glance to know it was my husband. I tried not to focus on his eyes, his purple prune-like skin, the hands that had once held mine. When I found the courage, I tried to gently wrap my hand around one of his hands and was overwhelmed by the cold, stiff and empty feeling my fingers felt. His lifeless body was just a shell; Drew's soul was in heaven now. He was the lucky one.

Drew's mother went in next. Moments later, I heard a bloodcurdling scream come from the room. My heart twisted for her. I could only imagine a mother's anguish. But what about me, his wife? I was grieving, too!

Drew's funeral was overwhelming, to say the least. Busloads of kids from other churches came to celebrate Drew's short life. The biggest church in town let us use their facility for the ceremony, and it was a good thing. It was standing room only. The pallbearers wore pink shirts instead of typical black ones, in honor of Drew's love for life. There were more flowers than I'd ever seen in one place. One worship song after another played; everyone joined in to sing. Drew's mom wailed from the front row. I stood by my parents and sister but felt so alone, trying to be brave.

"I'm so sorry. I can only imagine what you are going through."

"My deepest sympathies. I'm so sorry for your loss."

One by one, people filed before me, giving their condolences. I accepted them as graciously as possible, trying to look into eyes, shake hands and smile without breaking down. A few of them seemed awkward and insincere, but really, could I blame them? Some hardly knew Drew. Others, the ones with tear-stained faces, knew him well. But I was the one who knew him best. And while

they would all go back to their lives after this day, mine would be forever altered.

My sister drove me to the cemetery in her Mustang. I felt claustrophobic as the crowd charged toward me when we parked. "Hold on tight," my sister announced, putting the car into reverse. She plowed right over the grass and drove straight around the crowd.

"Thank you for that," I whispered, smiling sheepishly up at her. I could always count on my sister to have my back, even at moments like this.

Life went on, because it had to. I threw myself back into work and even got a promotion. From 9 to 5, I was a perky girl at the bank, clad in black slacks and high heels. But from evening on, I was a grieving widow, trying to figure out how to live without Drew. My family and a few very close friends fielded my phone calls and answered my door during this time, because I was too overwhelmed by well-meaning visitors. I needed to be alone with God, trying to figure things out.

Though my relationship with Drew's parents had always been a bit strained, I expected them to step up and comfort me during these difficult months. After all, we'd both lost someone we loved. But to my shock, his parents turned on me, treating me as if I had done something wrong, or worse, as if I hadn't been a part of his life.

"Why don't you just go find yourself a new husband online?" Drew's mother suggested flippantly one day.

*Excuse me?* I wanted to yell. Had I heard her incorrectly? Find a new husband? I didn't want a new one!

I wanted Drew, and I wanted them to be supportive. I needed someone to give me a hug, not tell me to get remarried.

Drew's sister, who had been very pregnant when he died, gave birth to a beautiful baby girl named Stephanie. I went to visit her at the hospital and tried to smile as this little blessing entered the world. "She's perfect," I whispered. But standing out in the hall, the tears began to fall. I leaned up against the wall and bawled uncontrollably. *That was supposed to be me, Lord! That was part of the plan, remember? A husband, a baby, a family. It was all I ever wanted.* And now my dream had been crushed, while someone else's dream lived on. The hurt stung in places I hadn't yet explored. Would it ever stop hurting?

I switched churches, hoping a fresh start might be just what I needed. My parents and sister were my rock during this time, constantly calling and visiting to check in on me. I sank into a deep depression; these were some of the darkest days of my life. I started taking antidepressants and waited for the sun to shine again, but there were only clouds. Suicide crossed my mind more than once. I grew angry, not with God, but with everyone around me. I couldn't believe the heartlessness of some of the people who had betrayed me; I wanted nothing to do with them.

Drew's parents' behavior grew more intolerable. Family members barged into my house on more than one occasion, trying to find and take Drew's belongings. His parents called me names, insisting that I was a spoiled brat. Every ounce of me wanted to shout back, "Forgive me for still wanting to hold onto my life!" But I didn't have the energy. I cried out to God, asking him to fight this battle for me, to help me forgive them for their hurtful behavior. I knew they were grieving, too, and taking out their heartbreak on me. But it still didn't feel fair.

I grew to love my new church but refused to get involved. I kept everyone at a safe distance, choosing to be an outsider. My once bubbly personality was bottled inside as I sat in the pew, half longing to sing in the worship team but knowing I wasn't anywhere near ready. I soon moved back home with my parents and returned to my home church, but I still refused to get involved. *Someday*, I told myself.

On the one-year anniversary of Drew's death, my aunt took me on a cruise off the Florida coast. I enjoyed the change of scenery and took in the fresh salty air, letting the sun kiss my cheeks. It was just what I needed.

On the way home, my mother called to ask how the trip had gone. "Kate, I've been thinking — you should join the worship team again," she encouraged me. "Your voice is a gift."

I agreed to get involved in that one thing, but I just wasn't ready to dive in. Instead, I dabbled with a new relationship, trying to make it work with everything I could, but my heart was still too raw. I wondered if I'd ever be ready to love and live again.

My cousin Michele, who is autistic, moved in with me for about a year and a half. I enjoyed taking care of her and realized how much I'd missed nurturing another person. I pursued my dream as a high school math teacher and wondered if I could make my life complete as a single person. One day, I finally gave it all up to God. "Lord, you know the desires of my heart. Since I was a little girl, all I've wanted was a family. But if this isn't what you have for me, if you want me to remain single, I accept that." I meant the words with all my heart. I had finally surrendered my dreams and desires to the one who gives and takes away.

And then one Sunday morning, not long after I prayed this prayer, a cute, muscular guy walked into church. I had to do a double take to realize it was my old childhood friend, Patrick. Our families had lived two doors down from each other growing up, and our mothers had been best friends and co-workers. Patrick and I had spent our summers fishing for crawdads down at the creek. We'd made many good memories, getting dirty, laughing and enjoying lazy summer afternoons outside. But we'd lost touch after high school when we went our own ways. Last I remembered, Patrick was somewhat of a rebel. And then there was me, with my perfect plans and straight A's.

I tried not to stare as Patrick sauntered toward me with a big grin on his face. Suddenly feeling self-conscious, I smoothed my hair and smiled back. This was the first time I really got to see him since Drew died.

"How are you?" he asked, his boyish voice now replaced with a man's.

I nodded. "Good!"

# TWO HEARTS

*Boy, you're cute!* I wanted to say. But I kept my cool. "Long time no see!"

We chatted for a few minutes, catching up on life. Patrick had gone off to the military. I had become a widow. We had both grown up. As I walked away that afternoon, I felt certain this wasn't the last I was going to see of my long lost childhood friend. And if I had looked back, I would have seen him looking after me, thinking the same.

ᢙᢙᢙ

## Patrick

From the time I was young, the military was a part of my life. My father served in the Navy for years but got out when I was 5 years old. Our family made our home in the small town of Kamiah, Idaho. Each Sunday, my parents took my sister, my brother and me to church, and I eagerly listened to stories about the Jesus of the Bible. I was a good kid, not getting into any more trouble than the next, but that soon changed when our family filed bankruptcy and was forced to move my eighth grade year. The timing could not have been worse. Just when my voice began to crack, so did my world.

We relocated to Kooskia for my father's work. Though just a few miles from my hometown, it felt like a foreign country. I tried to fit in with my new peers, but they weren't as accepting as I'd hoped. My grades began to slip, an obvious sign of my unhappiness. The kids at school picked on me relentlessly, making junior high miserable.

One morning, a tall boy with a sneer came toward me, shoving me against his locker with such force that I saw stars. He then sauntered away, high-fiving his friends as he laughed.

I brushed myself off and kept on walking. I hated school. I hated my new town, and I hated everyone here. What sort of cruel punishment was this, moving an awkward adolescent kid during his second year of junior high?

Wanting somewhere to belong, I decided to join the basketball team. It seemed to ease the loneliness for a while. Staying busy, however, wasn't enough to keep me out of trouble.

The end of eighth grade year, I snuck out to my first party thinking it would be fun. I was always complaining about my lack of friends; perhaps this would be a great way to meet people and enjoy myself.

The party was hopping when I arrived. A group of guys huddled by the bonfire. Surprisingly, they made an effort to say hello. The booze flowed freely, and I joined in, not wanting to be a dud. Music blared in the background, while a crackling fire served as the centerpiece to a drunken fest.

"Hey, man, good to see you!" A guy from my math class waved with his beer bottle, stumbling over to me with bloodshot eyes. "Ready to hang with the big boys, huh?"

# TWO HEARTS

"Yeah, sure," I mumbled, taking a long swig of my own beer. It wasn't too nasty. "Good to see you, too." I scanned the place for cute chicks and was pleasantly surprised to see there were several. Maybe I *had* been missing out!

"You gonna get laid tonight?" the guy asked, nudging me with a wink.

I felt my cheeks go red. "Maybe."

"Well, good luck with that." He laughed and stumbled off, nearly falling into the fire pit as he approached a pretty girl. I watched as he leaned in to flatter her, watched as she batted her lashes and pulled him away with her moments later. Well, *he* obviously didn't need any luck tonight.

By the time I was 15, I had lost my virginity and was partying hard. I still attended church most Sundays and vowed each week to be a better person but found myself slipping right back into my ways when Monday rolled around. My grades dropped below a 2.0 GPA, and most people thought I'd never get into college if I kept things up.

I pulled my grades up my junior year and found work at a local grocery store. My days were filled with work, school, wrestling practice and partying. I was the average all-American high school boy to most, but inside, I knew something was missing.

My relationship with God had been put on the back burner, replaced by the enticements of this world. As much as I knew I needed to get back on track, I was simply having too much fun. (In fact, I was having so much fun

# SINK OR SWIM

— or so I thought — that in the middle of all of this fun my best friend got my girlfriend pregnant. But, I didn't know that until much later.)

After graduation, I did a year of college, but it didn't work out for me so well. I moved back home to work for the summer and began dating a girl named Emily. She was pretty and fun and seemed to dig me pretty hard. She had a baby from a previous relationship, and I hoped I could be some sort of role model to the boy. Emily and I got engaged and married shortly after that. College was now out of the question for me; I had a family to raise. I was excited to be a new husband and determined to make a good life for Emily and her son. Perhaps, if we were lucky, we would add our own children to the mix.

A week after we were married, I heard a rumor that Emily was cheating on me with her baby's daddy. I confronted her about it, and she insisted she didn't sleep with him. Later, however, she admitted to her affair.

"I'm so sorry, Patrick. Please forgive me. I won't do it again," she pleaded.

I was heartbroken but chose to believe her. My parents had been strong role models for me growing up, and I didn't believe in divorce. I would remain faithful to Emily and hope she would do the same for me.

Because I didn't finish college, I floundered in keeping a consistent job, going from one to the next. I found work at a Potlatch mill doing cleanup for $10 an hour. It wasn't great pay, but for someone without an education, it was better than nothing. I wanted to provide for my wife so she could stay home with the baby and take care of our home.

One evening, while working, I suddenly had a terrible feeling that Emily was cheating on me. I left early that night and rushed home, half expecting to find her in our bed with another man. While she wasn't, she did confess a week or two later that she'd been sleeping with someone else.

I didn't say much that day, but my feelings were deeply hurt; my pride was wounded as well. I continued to drink and smoke two packs of cigarettes a day and tried focusing on my work. I was at a crossroads; I could divorce Emily or love her through our struggles. I chose to try to make things work. We sought out counseling from my old pastor back home, but nothing seemed to work. We continued in a destructive cycle, her cheating and both of us partying. Deep in my heart, I knew I needed to fully give my life and my situation over to God, but instead of trusting in him, I tried to take matters into my own hands. And things continued to go downhill.

One morning, I was driving to work when Emily called, her voice oozing with fury. "Why did your mom call my mom to tell her I was going to pick up James from jail?" she screamed. James was a recent fling of Emily's.

I sighed and attempted to defend myself. "Look, Emily, I'm sick of all this, so you can either straighten up and quit cheating on me for good or get out."

"I want out!" Emily screamed and slammed down the phone.

# SINK OR SWIM

Tears burned my eyes as I stared at my phone. I tried to focus on work that day, but it was difficult to do. The next day, Emily called again.

"You can come over and get your stuff while I'm at work," I told her matter-of-factly.

That night, when I returned home, I found she'd torn up all of our photos and strewn the pieces around the house, leaving a giant mess on our living room floor. I picked up a broom and swept up the pieces, tossing my heart out along with the debris.

I had tried everything possible to salvage our relationship, but my marriage had still failed. I threw myself into my work but was too distracted to be of much good. I eventually got laid off and went back to work at the grocery store. The days and nights blurred together into one sad existence. I hit a new low point and wondered how much longer I could go on like this, weaving in and out of meaningless jobs and living without purpose or hope. I retreated to smoking and drinking, trying to drown out my sorrows.

One night, I hit my pillow and cried out to God. "Lord, I'm sorry. I know I haven't always done the right thing. I'm asking for your forgiveness and a fresh start in my life. I'm burned out and have nowhere else to go. Please show me what to do," I prayed desperately. My heart, though so hollow and sad, still hung onto the hope that God might have a good plan for my life someday.

"Have you ever considered the military?" my boss asked me one day out of the blue.

# TWO HEARTS

"Not really," I replied, shrugging, and that was about all of the conversation.

Something inside of me jumped, though. Several other people had mentioned the military to me in the past few weeks, and suddenly, it seemed like the right thing to do. I asked my mom, dad, sister and brother and everyone else that I could think of to talk to at the time, and I prayed about it for a couple of weeks. "Okay, God, I know this is what you want me to do," I prayed at last. "The military it is." Excitement mounted in me at the thought of pursuing this new adventure. I researched the Air Force and joined shortly after.

For most new recruits, boot camp is grueling, but for me, it was pure hell. I'd already hit the lowest point in my life, and being woken up several times a night to people yelling at me was not the easiest situation. Three weeks into boot camp, I started to snap out of my misery and chose to embrace my new life. With each pushup and jumping jack, I became more determined to be the best I could be. I may have been a failure up until now, but things were about to change. I was about to become a new man.

I went on to tech school, where my grades put me at the top of my class. Shortly after, I was stationed in Mountain Home, Idaho, just outside Boise. The flat, bare terrain was quite a contrast from my beautiful green hometown of Kamiah, but I made the most of my time there. Three months after the move, I chose to give up my two-pack-a-day smoking habit cold turkey. I quit drinking once and for all, and with God's help, I gave up sleeping around, too.

One day, I sat in my dorm room alone and had a heart-to-heart with God. "Lord, I want to devote my life to what you want and not what I want," I prayed. "You know best, and I'm going to stop looking to women to fulfill the empty space in my heart. Instead, I'm going to fill that space with you. Thank you, God, for dying on the cross for my sins and forgiving me despite the unthinkable things I've done. If I never have another girlfriend or get married again, my life is still yours to do as you please. I am done drinking, smoking and sleeping around. I've tried to commit my life fully to you before but have always failed miserably. It's taken me going down a pretty rocky road to get to this place, and I'm fully ready to give my life to you." A peace I hadn't felt in some time washed over me as I finished my prayer.

Shortly after I made the decision to turn my life around, I took leave from the military and attended a Christian men's conference at The Life Center Church in Kamiah, where I grew even closer to the Lord. As the speaker read from the Bible and prayed with us, I felt a new sense of hope and peace wash over me. Like everyone else, I had fallen into sin and been hurt by the world, but by God's grace, I had been forgiven. How refreshing it was to know that nothing could separate me from his love!

During the conference, I saw a familiar face on the worship team. It was Kate, my old childhood friend. She had turned into the most beautiful woman that I had ever seen; in fact, she barely resembled the little girl I'd once caught crawdads with in the creek out behind our house. I made a point to talk to her after church and hoped I didn't blush as we caught up on our lives. I felt sad to hear she'd been widowed; I had met Drew several years before and had even attended their wedding. It seemed life had been tough for both of us.

As Kate walked away that afternoon, I hoped it wouldn't be the last I'd be seeing of her. And I wondered if she felt the same.

ትትት

### Kate

"I'm never getting married again!" I declared as I hopped off my four-wheeler and brushed the dirt off my knees.

"Me neither!" Patrick agreed with a laugh, parking his four-wheeler next to mine. "Man, that was fun! It's too bad everyone else missed out!"

"Yeah, it's too bad." Several of our friends had organized a four-wheeling event one Saturday, but at the last minute, everyone else canceled, leaving Patrick and me to venture out alone. Secretly, I wondered if that hadn't been such a bad thing. We'd had a blast riding up and down the forest paths on our four-wheelers, kicking up dirt and discussing our future plans that included anything but marriage. Patrick had been burned in his marriage and had decided bachelor life was the way to go.

Upon his arrival back in Idaho, Patrick and I had rekindled our old childhood friendship. I was pleased to see he had grown into such a ruggedly good-looking guy. I had put on some weight after Drew's death and feared Patrick was probably out of my league, so I hadn't much thought about the attraction being mutual. Still, it had been nice to catch up with Patrick like no time had passed at all. He seemed so much more like the boy I had known in our youth and much less like the rebellious guy in high school who'd preferred partying over studying. I could see that God had done a great deal of work in Patrick's life and that he truly wanted to serve him now.

Patrick returned to his base at Mountain Home, but we continued to talk on a regular basis. The next weekend, he asked me out on a real date. I spent forever fussing in the mirror, hoping a little lip gloss and mascara would help shake off the last of Patrick's memories of me as a get-down-in-the-dirt childhood pal. From the look on his face when he picked me up, I was pretty sure he no longer saw me as the girl next door.

"I bought these for you," Patrick announced, pulling a gorgeous bouquet of expensive red roses from his truck, which I accepted gratefully.

"Thank you," I gushed. "They're beautiful!"

We spent the day driving around, taking walks and talking about everything under the sun. I knew I was falling for Patrick, and it seemed he felt the same way. Still, were things moving too quickly? We'd both been hurt before; should we take things more slowly? Part of me said yes, but my heart screamed, *Go for it! You've known him your whole life! Isn't that long enough?*

At the end of the day, Patrick pulled me close for our first kiss. Our conversation from two days earlier, during which I'd asked him where things were going, came to my mind: "I'm going to marry you someday, Kate. God told me so, but I'm just waiting for you to be ready."

I melted in his arms. Here was the boy of my youth, the one who had vehemently declared he was never getting married again, now practically proposing. And the crazy thing was I wanted to marry him, too.

Not long after our date, Patrick proposed to me over dinner at the Olive Garden restaurant. As curious onlookers watched, he dropped to one knee and popped the question. "Kate, will you marry me?"

As I looked into those too-familiar eyes, my own welled with tears. Nothing had ever seemed so right in my life. "Of course I will," I replied without hesitation.

Patrick was deployed overseas for the next six months. We planned our wedding while keeping in touch through short phone calls, encouraging each other to hang in there because we'd soon be together forever. Patrick spent this time poring over his Bible, growing closer to the Lord and praying for strength to become the godly husband he wanted to be. I struggled with insecurity and fear while he was gone, but once again, God reminded me to trust in him.

Patrick and I were married on May 31, 2008 in a

beautiful ceremony by the creek we played in as kids. I had pictured this day many times in my mind, wondering if I would somehow feel I was betraying Drew's memory by marrying someone else. At that moment, however, with the sun beating down on my face, I felt as if Drew was looking down from heaven, cheering me on with the rest of the happy guests. As much as I'd loved Drew, a part of me deep down had always felt he wasn't the one I was meant to grow old with. I'd never spoken that thought out loud, but now it all made sense. I was meant to grow old with Patrick, the one I'd known all my life, the one who'd been right under my nose all along.

Patrick and I bought a 40 x 12 trailer and affectionately named it The Love Shack. We began to try for a baby, but I didn't get pregnant right away as I'd expected. Once again, God reminded me that my plans and his are sometimes two different things. He also reminded me that his timing is perfect, his ways are better and that trusting in him is always the best route to go.

A verse popped into my mind one day several months after Patrick and I had been trying: "Delight yourself in the Lord and he will give you the desires of your heart" (Psalm 37:4).

*Lord, I want you to be my true delight. I pray that you will give me the desire of my heart in your perfect timing.* And I left it at that and decided to trust.

On August 5, 2009, a beautiful little boy, whom we named Christopher, came into the world, bright pink and weighing a perfect 6 pounds, 10 ounces. I marveled at his tiny features and gave thanks to the Lord, who had indeed given me the deepest desires of my heart. Patrick, who had been scheduled to deploy overseas, had been able to stay home to see his new son's birth. We praised God for yet another miracle, for allowing us to all be together during these precious first few days of our son's life.

"I feel like the luckiest guy on earth," Patrick whispered as he took Christopher's miniature finger in his grip.

"You are," I giggled. I felt pretty lucky, too. But really, I knew it was more than luck. It was God's grace and nothing more that had gotten us where we were today. Through tragedy and painful heartache, God had restored both of our lives. He had mended our broken hearts, weaving them together as though they were meant all along. I could not have asked for more.

જ્જ્જ્

"What do two pink lines mean?" Patrick asked casually as he scooped Christopher, now 6 months old, from my arms and planted a big kiss on his head.

"What?!" I raced over to see if my husband was correct.

"Two pink lines," Patrick repeated.

I laughed out loud as I stared at the little pregnancy test stick that bore two pink lines. "We're having another baby!"

I waited, half expecting Patrick to faint or run for the

hills. But he just jumped for joy. Since moving to a base in Portugal, our lives had changed quite dramatically. Life on base in a foreign country had been quite an adjustment, but we had grown to love our new community, church and friends overseas. Baby number two was coming a bit sooner than planned, but as I'd already learned, life rarely goes as planned.

"That's awesome!" he said enthusiastically, hoisting Christopher onto his shoulders. "Maybe it will be twins!"

"Ha ha." I patted my belly and wondered if he might be right. Wouldn't that be something!

God had been so good to us the past few years. Not only was our marriage thriving, but my heart was healing as well. Though Drew's parents had been very hurtful to me for years, I learned to forgive them with God's help. It was not an easy process, but it was a choice, and every day I asked God for the strength to love them as he did. Drew's sister apologized for her family's behavior, and God fully restored our relationship. Drew would always remain a part of my past and my heart, but my future was with Patrick.

As much as we had come to enjoy Portugal, we could hardly wait to return home to Idaho. Kamiah seemed the only logical place on earth to raise our family. After all, it was where Patrick and my story first began.

We also looked forward to returning to The Life Center, the church that had played such an integral part in my healing after Drew's death. Never in my life had I felt so at home and so loved as I had when I stepped in the doors of The Life Center. The people were family to me, and I couldn't wait to reunite with them and share more stories of God's goodness in our lives.

As Christopher and Patrick played, I sank onto the couch and took it all in, enjoying every laugh and squeal. My mind drifted to the girl of my youth and her plans. I was going to take on the world back then. But, oh, how life had set me straight. Through much heartache, I had learned that only God can determine our paths, but in the end, his path is the best one to be on. I'd also learned to give over the desires of my heart to him. In his perfect timing, he fulfills those desires as he sees best. We may not have it all figured out, but he does, and I'm going to plan on trusting him.

# SAUNDRA'S TREASURE
## THE STORY OF SAUNDRA
### WRITTEN BY CHRISTEE WISE

"We've done this before, haven't we?" my friend Jayce asked casually as I waited for him in his living room in Bellingham. He pressed a plastic bag of white powder and some small squares of paper with his thumb against a circular mirror about eight inches across in his right hand. Motioning toward me with the paraphernalia, he invited my answer with a shrug.

"Uh-uh." I shook my head. I had watched my friend Gina suck a line of cocaine up her nose a few times and witnessed her bizarre, detached behavior afterward. To me, it was disgusting, and I swore I'd never do it.

I now observed Jayce carefully setting the pieces out on the coffee table as if he was about to serve us dinner. He was my man of the hour. We had been friends for a couple years, and I trusted him. Today, he was a hero who had rescued me from Ryan, my creepy ex who'd been stalking me for a couple weeks.

The incessant beeping and throbbing of my cell phone kept me on edge all weekend. I'd stopped answering it, but Ryan would hang up and try again a few minutes later. I ran to Jayce for help.

I complained, "Ryan just doesn't get it. I'm done with him. He just won't let go."

# SINK OR SWIM

The relationship I'd had with Ryan was like all the others. We'd been intimate within hours of meeting at a party. I couldn't seem to relate to men any other way. Afterward, I might get to know them, but it was always too late. Jayce was an exception, a kind of friend with benefits.

But Ryan was especially needy. The relationship had stretched several weeks longer than usual, when I decided to call it quits. He reacted fervidly. "It can't be over. You haven't even given us a try," he whined. He emailed and called. He waited outside my house and at Kinko's for me to get off work.

Several times I gave in to his tantrums because he threatened to commit suicide. Finally, I couldn't take it any longer. "You will be fine," I told him frankly. I tried reasoning. "You don't want to be with someone who doesn't care for you the way you care for them."

He persisted.

Finally, when my cell phone rang nonstop for an hour, Jayce grabbed it. "Listen, dude. She told you it's over. What don't you understand?"

I could tell by his smug expression that Ryan was stunned. I overheard my ex's angry tirade.

"Yes, she's with me, and she doesn't want to talk to you or see you again," Jayce replied fiercely.

Hearing Jayce say that we were together, even if it was only for a night, sent a gratifying current through me. No man had ever stood by me.

I jumped when Jayce snapped the phone shut. My nerves were shot, and I was trembling with anger. Tossing the phone toward me, he slammed his hands on his thighs and lunged from the couch. He left the room and came back with the cocaine.

"You want to?" He grinned and held the little bag up for me to see. He sat down again, and I scooted up to the edge of his sofa.

I glanced from the bag to Jayce's face to the table and back. His hazel eyes and disheveled blond hair seemed more attractive than before. I wanted to believe that he liked me. I wanted to forget Ryan and all the rest. I wanted to please Jayce. I wanted him to see that I accepted him so that he would accept me.

The mirror caught our reflection and held it briefly, just about as long as I took to think about what I was about to do.

"Heck, yeah!" I answered, eager to prolong the pleasure of Jayce's attentiveness.

I watched as he tapped out three little ridges of chalky white from the corner of the plastic bag across the mirror. He handed me a paper square, and with practiced skill, he rolled his own into a straw. Then he leaned over and smoothly ingested the first strip of powder through the tube and into his nose and senses. He sniffed and pinched his nose with cool satisfaction and winked at me. He nodded and gave me an encouraging smile. His pupils grew large. The coke was having its effect.

Nervously, I bent down and angled my "straw" between my nostril and the row of dust. Pausing over my first draw of cocaine, I saw myself in the mirror. The brown-haired 26 year old that stared fearfully back closed her eyes in shame.

Moments later, nervousness and shame were forgotten. The situation with Ryan was forgotten. The euphoric effect of cocaine on my system shoved every negative thought and feeling I had of myself aside as well.

"Feels good, huh?" Jayce laughed.

"Mmm-hmm," I joined him.

I could not remember the last time I felt good about myself.

❧❧❧

Encircled in my father's arms, I stood at the front of New Life Chapel in Kamiah, Idaho. At 5 years old, I barely understood what I was doing. Everyone was singing, and some of the ladies were crying.

The kind man our family called Pastor Bomley walked back and forth on the stage. I liked Pastor Bomley a lot, but when he stood in front of the crowd and talked for an especially long time, I could not pay attention. Once in a while, I heard words I'd heard in Sunday school. "Jesus" was the most familiar one.

Jesus was a browned-haired, bearded man in a white robe with a long blue scarf. In the picture that hung in our classroom, Jesus sat on a rock, smiling warmly with some children like me gathered around him. Warm contentment filled me at the thought of being accepted by such an important man. I had heard "Jesus is the son of

# SAUNDRA'S TREASURE

God" and supposed it to be a fact. I didn't know what that meant, only that this man who lived a long, long time ago was very, very special.

When Pastor Bomley said, "Raise your hand," I raised my hand.

When he said, "Come to the front of the church, and I will pray for you," the crowd rustled and several people stood up and moved to the aisles.

"Excuse me, excuse me," I heard from the row behind me. I looked up at my daddy.

"Can we go?" I asked.

Daddy took my hand, and we walked to the front of the church. Led by the preacher to "accept Jesus into my heart" by repeating his prayer words, I was glad to hear my daddy's big voice saying them, too.

"Amen," we all said together. Daddy gave me a little squeeze. I felt happy, contented, loved and a little bit different. Most of all, I had the idea that when I had "let Jesus come into my heart," that I'd been admitted into some very big and wonderful club of belonging. I was accepted and special, as if a tiny gem had been placed inside me.

Daddy worked long hours. When he was home, I wanted to be with him all of the time. I loved being outside. I was happy to trail him wherever he went, watching, helping or pretending to do whatever it was he was doing. If he was working on the car, I was under there with him. If he was working in his shop, I'd be there handing him tools or just treasuring our time together.

# SINK OR SWIM

Janetta, my older sister by five years, and I were as different as night and day. She was reserved and quiet, even shy. She preferred to stay in her room to read or listen to music. Janetta never seemed to mind being alone, but I feared I might end up without a group in which I belonged.

❧❧❧

Fear began to stalk me as I approached eighth grade graduation and high school. Next to other girls, I felt plain. None of the guys seemed interested in more than friendship.

My closest friend Julie was pretty and gifted and especially good. I never felt as if I measured up to the standards of Julie or Janetta. After awhile, I based decisions on whether or not it was something Julie or Janetta would consider. If they were too good to engage in a certain activity, then I would do it just because I could be more daring.

By the time I was 16, I was completely convinced the only thing I might have to offer to capture or hold a guy's interest was sex. Who or what had given me that notion, I wasn't sure, but it was as firmly implanted in my brain as the law of gravity.

I wanted someone like Tyler to like me as more than a friend. How could I make that happen? Throughout my junior year, I set everything else aside, thinking about and befriending him.

# SAUNDRA'S TREASURE

"So how about tomorrow?" Tyler suggested.

I looked across the table at the object of my distraction. Tyler's mild interest in me, no matter his motive, attracted me even more than his striking looks. He had graduated, and I was surprised that we were still spending time together now that school was out.

Tall and thin, Tyler had mischievous brown hair that balanced the sharp angles of his face. His icy-blue eyes were soft, betraying a bruised heart, and I felt sorry for him knowing he didn't have it easy at home. I had to stop mid-daydream to remind myself that Tyler was totally out of my league.

"Yeah, sure," I answered casually. My answer amazed me as much as his suggestion that we have sex, even though we'd talked about it some already. I'd planned to save myself for marriage. I was raised believing it was the right thing to do.

*No one is standing in line for me. He wants me, why shouldn't I give myself to him?*

We met at a friend's house the next day. Tyler led me down to the basement as if he'd been there before. The room was unfinished, cool but not uncomfortably so. My eyes adjusted slowly to the light that filtered through a small square of window in a corner far from the stairs. I spotted a makeshift daybed in the darkest corner just as Tyler took my hand and pulled me toward it.

Within days of losing my virginity, disappointment in myself danced on the surface of my awareness. I dismissed the broken promise and tried to commit to memory the acceptance and belonging I had found in being with Tyler.

To my humiliation, some of the guys from our group of friends came to me the next day. They each leaned over my shoulder and repeated verbatim words Tyler had said to me during our tryst.

Our friendship cooled afterward. I saw less and less of Tyler that summer. In the fall, he joined the Navy, and I began my senior year.

I had a terrible basketball season. The coach told me I was slacking. I'd lost interest and confidence in myself, and I ended up quitting track and softball.

A classmate, Aaron, began inviting me to his house regularly. Aaron always had a steady girlfriend, but kept me on the side. I was there for him in case she didn't give him what he wanted. I got used to the pattern.

By the time I graduated from high school, I'd grown desperate to get out from under my parents' strict standards. My sister, Janetta, had a place of her own just across town. Irresistible freedom beckoned me at 18.

"You can live with me as long as you pay part of the rent and help with groceries," she offered firmly.

As shy and unsure as she was with others, she stood her ground with me. Her faith and values were decided. I admired her for that, but I knew I could never be as good as Janetta.

A part-time job allowed me to keep my end of the bargain. Janetta and I did grow closer. After rejecting the church throughout my senior year, I attended again with my sister. Living side by side, though, our profound differences flashed. Every so often, I'd stumble in late at night after partying with friends.

"You know better, Saundra," Janetta would say. She tried hard to make me listen. "You are making bad choices. I'm concerned about you."

"I'm concerned for you, too," I said, deflecting her words and my conscience. "You need to get out and have some fun … make some friends, sis." And then one day I introduced her to Derek.

After a year, I jumped at a chance to move to the East Coast to be a nanny. I'd always loved kids. Adventurous and independent, I had no fear of making the cross-country move. The shocking difference in culture from the little reservation town where I'd lived my entire life sent me reeling.

Two weeks after I arrived, I called my parents. "Mom, I want to come home."

"I understand, honey, but you made a commitment," my mother maintained.

I turned back to God in my time of need, hoping that by going to church I'd find some strength and comfort. Since I had no transportation, my employers dictated the church I attended. Their choice and those within walking distance of the house were a poor fit for me.

One week I had the chance to attend the church that was founded by David Wilkerson, the author of *The Cross and the Switchblade*. The pastor spoke about real people with real problems and a loving, caring God that I, at that moment, could only hope was real. I didn't know how to pray and feared that I had already blown my chance with God.

I was drawn to that church but could only get back there a couple times over the next few months.

Sadness and depression darkened my thoughts and swallowed me in isolation and loneliness. The infrequent nights I went out with friends, I stayed out all night drinking to fit in with them and to forget.

"Saundra! We're getting married." Janetta's happy news instantly brightened my day. Even though I had been sure that I'd be the first one married, I was happily surprised to hear that my beautiful but quiet sister was engaged.

The wedding gave me something to look forward to and an excuse to terminate my career as a nanny in New York. With delight, I zipped my suitcase shut for the last time, closing the most horrible year of my life. I boarded the plane and promised myself I'd never look back.

After the wedding, I moved to Iowa to spend some time with my grandmother. For the first time, I was on my own. I didn't have employers or family watching over my every move and telling me what I could and couldn't do. I partied and dated freely.

I met Kevin at work. He was one of the nicest guys I'd ever met because he truly wanted to get to know me as a person. I had no idea how to have a healthy relationship. The thought terrified me.

My grandmother's passing suspended my thoughts of a future with Kevin. Then shortly after, another call from my sister clinched my decision to leave Iowa.

My beautiful niece, Andrea, was born several weeks premature with numerous medical complications and a very unpredictable future. I checked in with Janetta and Derek frequently long distance. Hearing the stress and fatigue in their voices, I knew I had to go.

Kevin came out to visit me in Washington. He met my sister's family. We went to the coast and spent several special days together. But Kevin wasn't planning on leaving Iowa, and I wasn't interested in going back. The relationship faded.

Before long, I had a job and was making friends in the Bellingham area. My sister couldn't hide her concern over my reckless lifestyle, but didn't know what to do with me, either. The only thing she could do was prevent me from seeing Andrea if she detected smoke or alcohol on me.

I complied by keeping my two lives separate.

Two lives became three when I began seeing a married man.

Up until then, I had sworn I'd never get involved with a married man. Approaching my mid-20s, life began to speed up drastically. I loved my sister's family with all my heart, but after five years of watching from the outside, I wanted to be on the inside. Ed opened the door to let me in. Sixteen years older than me, a police officer and a well-known citizen, I couldn't imagine what he saw in me. Of course, I was just his mistress and would never be anything more. I favored this interest he had in me over nothing at all and carried on with him, welcoming his advances, attention and gifts. I was never drunk or wasted when I was with Ed. He encouraged me to work out, met me at the gym and promoted self-respect through fitness. The irony that he was taking complete advantage of me never fazed me.

The erosion of my self-worth was almost complete. I had bartered most of my values for a chance to belong. Secrecy and crack would take what remained.

My best friend Kat never knew about Ed. Neither did Jayce or his best friend Trevor. Ed never knew about them, and Janetta didn't know anything about anything. Kat didn't touch drugs and wouldn't want anything to do with me if she ever found out I had done them. Jayce introduced me to snorting cocaine, but I hadn't seen him smoke it. I raised this as a new limit.

Furtive binges with friends, alcohol and sex turned into routines with each line I crossed. I started taking more chances.

Kat and I landed at Jayce's house one day after having several drinks. The acceptance I felt with my friends intoxicated me. I could not say no to them. I quickly adjusted my standards and gave myself to them both.

Kat got up to go to the bathroom, and Jayce turned to me. He pulled out his crack pipe and offered me some. *Movie stars and rich people snort coke,* I had thought, *but addicts smoke crack in back alleys.*

I reached out and took the cylinder from Jayce. I hardly recognized myself anymore.

On the outside, I remained a decent and trustworthy

# SAUNDRA'S TREASURE

20-something. A former boss trusted me enough to invite me to housesit for her while she was away. I'd had many people ask me to do the same thing for them.

Shortly after she turned over the keys, Trevor and Jayce showed up on the doorstep. I invited them in, intending only to have drinks and a hit of the drug I'd come to look forward to. The next day, I recalled getting high and having sex with both of them. I wondered how I could so callously abuse the privilege and trust she had that I'd respect her beautiful home.

I caught up with my friends Mick and Teresa a few weeks later at a wedding reception. The three of us frequented the open bar, loosened up and began to enjoy each other's company. Teresa laughed as her husband, Mick, and I flirted brazenly. She hung on both of us and invited me to come home with them.

Behind the closed doors of their apartment, innuendo became suggestion of a threesome. I felt sick but laughed, as if they were joking. They were drunk, but serious, and I was outnumbered. I couldn't seem to excuse myself.

Afterward, I stayed in the shower washing myself until the water ran cold.

Oddly, I now relied upon the affair with Ed for a sense of normality.

The next Friday, Kat and I went barhopping late after work. After closing down the last place, we staggered outside and down the street, passing several knots of people. We noticed a young man standing in the shadows.

Kat pulled me toward him. "Hi, what's your name?"

# SINK OR SWIM

He wore jeans and a t-shirt with a patriotic slogan and a military logo. "PFC Lawrence," he said quietly. He looked us over and smiled curiously. We spent several minutes talking with him.

"Is Lawrence your first name or your last name?" Kat asked, snuggling up to him.

"Well, I don't know if I can tell you," he teased. He put his arm around her and reached his other out to me.

I was awkward, even a little scared at picking up a total stranger. I'd messed around plenty the past few years, but only with people I knew at least a little bit. And, in all of my drunken sexual escapades, I never used any kind of protection against pregnancy or disease.

All of a sudden, I felt especially dirty and desperate, nearly overcome with an urge to run. *I can't leave Kat*, I thought.

I tried to catch my friend's attention. She ignored me.

I kept asking myself over and over that night, "What have I done to myself? What have I done?"

The next day, I woke up sober and gripped with fear. Inside my heart, I realized I had gone way too far. I had to get out.

I gave my two weeks' notice at work. I met Ed for the last time to tell him I was leaving. He hugged me and told me, "Take care."

Then, I ran for the safety of Kamiah. I didn't know what was there for me, but I knew that it was the only way out of the affair, the drugs and the dangerous friendships I'd formed.

# SAUNDRA'S TREASURE

I happily connected with one of my best friends from high school, Liz-Beth, soon after I came back. We'd always hit it off. Liz-Beth, I knew, accepted me just as I was. I loved that I could be myself with her.

One evening just weeks after I'd moved back to Kamiah, Liz-Beth and I ran out to the only place that was open, the Casino, to buy cigarettes.

Moments later, Liz-Beth's brother pulled his truck into the parking lot nearby.

"Is that Lucas?" I gasped.

"He had such a crush on you back in high school," Liz-Beth laughed.

"Really?" A surge of happy excitement coursed through me. Secretly, I wanted to hear her say it again. I could never have dreamed in high school that someone like Lucas, whom I thought was so cute, even noticed me. He may have been three years younger, Liz-Beth's little brother, but any girl in school would have given anything to be his girlfriend. I'd never told anyone that it was I who had a crush on Lucas back then, nor did I tell Liz-Beth now.

While I'd been gone, Lucas had graduated, gotten married and had two kids. The grown-up Lucas was as attractive as ever to me. Quickly, I dismissed the enticing thoughts, reminding myself he was married.

When he called a few days later, I rationalized based on Liz-Beth's endorsement.

*He's been separated for two years. The marriage is over.*

# SINK OR SWIM

Lucas was one of only two or three men who didn't expect or get sex right away. I couldn't believe it when he politely said good night after our first date.

He was a wonderful single father to his children, who lived with him most of the time. I couldn't keep myself from falling for him.

After a few weeks, we were sharing a house and a bed, and he'd begun the paperwork for a divorce.

❧❧❧

"I'm hungry." Five-year-old Joshua pulled on my arm. I looked down at his enormous brown eyes.

"Me, too," Mikayla chimed in, always right behind her big brother.

The baby inside of me karate-chopped my own growling stomach, as if to remind me that I needed to eat for us both very soon.

I'd stretched the oatmeal, eggs and potatoes as far as I could and divided the last of the milk evenly between the children's cups that morning for breakfast. The clock read almost 2 p.m., and I longed to have a decent meal on the table by the time Lucas arrived home from work. The refrigerator and the kitchen cabinets were empty, though. We had no money.

"I know." I laid a hand on top of each child's head and pulled them gently to my sides. Joshua had his father's stout build. I could feel his strength in the resistance against the palm of my hand. But he yielded to my affectionate touch, and both children leaned hard against me.

Lucas' children were beautiful and sweet kids. Even though we'd been together less than a year, I already loved them as if they were my own. They both had the dark hair and eyes of the Native American heritage I found so attractive in their dad. I hoped our baby would look like its father. I hoped we'd belong.

*I have to get some food,* my maternal instincts demanded. *The kids need milk, and I need something to keep my strength up for the baby's sake.*

I was seven months pregnant. I hadn't done drugs since I left Bellingham, and the day I found out I was pregnant was the day I stopped smoking and drinking.

Lightheaded and weak, I now approached the driveway of The Life Center Church. A strange, surreal feeling enveloped me as I paused to stare at the entrance to the food pantry.

This was not the church building that I'd attended as a child. Two churches had joined together while I was gone, and they had a new pastor and a new building. Yet I couldn't shake the mix of relief and fear I sensed that I somehow was coming home. I was sure that what I'd done in my life was not up to church standards. I was equally sure that everyone could see every last one of my sins displayed boldly in flashing lights above my head, or at least on my protruding belly.

The only thing that pushed me beyond my embarrassment was our hunger.

# SINK OR SWIM

"Saundra? Is that you?" To my dreaded surprise, the first woman to see me when I walked into the food pantry at The Life Center recognized me immediately.

My face grew red-hot, and I strained to get a one-word answer out: "Yes."

"Oh, my goodness, you are all grown up. And look at your children!" The woman whose face I remembered clearly, but whose name I'd forgotten, threw her arms around me and gave me a hug. She bubbled on about me and my parents and my sister and then pulled me around to introduce me to the new pastor.

Pastor Kelly shook my hand and welcomed me. I thanked him politely but could think of nothing else to say. I couldn't even explain to Gloria, as he called her, that these were not actually my very own children or that I wasn't married to my baby's father.

Mikayla began to pull on my arm and point at the stacks of Campbell's soup she recognized on the food pantry shelves. Joshua had already picked out a box of cereal thinking he was in a regular grocery store.

As I started to corral the kids, suddenly Gloria returned to the present. "Oh, goodness. Let them pick out what they want. Here." She shoved a large cardboard carton into my arms. "What do you need?"

I left that day with a carload of staples and a strong desire to go back for something more than food.

"I'd really like to go back to that church," I told Lucas. "The people there just seemed to really care."

We visited the church a few weeks later. To my

surprise, we were welcomed as if we'd been sitting on the front row for the past 30 years.

We went several more times before Timothy was born in August of 2007.

I still felt ashamed to attend church when we weren't married but living together. Our relationship was complicated by many issues. Pastor Kelly offered to counsel us and spent many hours talking with us free of charge.

I never felt condemned or pressured. The people of the church continued to love and accept us. My heart was touched and comforted to find out that Pastor Bomley, who led me to Jesus at 5 years old, still attended the church.

The next August, Lucas and I went to the Justice of the Peace. Our parents were there, and in the simplest of ceremonies, we were married.

My past continued to raise its ugly head and cause pain in the marriage. More frequently in my mind than on my husband's lips, the accusations echoed. *You gave yourself so easily to strangers, why don't you want to give yourself to your husband, to one who treats you well?*

No one could ever understand how awful I felt and how much I wished to reclaim my purity and give it to the one man who truly loved me. I loathed my history and had disengaged body and emotion almost entirely. The old lies were still deeply burned in my heart and mind. Now I battled new thoughts: *You can't undo the past. You are what you are — undeserving, unforgiveable.*

# SINK OR SWIM

Though we attended church, I could not stop the tapes that replayed in my head. Eventually, I began to slip in my faith. Lucas and I were fighting more often. Our life got busy, and we started missing church. My past still haunted me. Deep depression, which runs in my family, clouded my thinking, and condemnation continually hammered my heart.

Through this, though, I truly enjoyed my job as an office assistant at a busy accounting firm in town. A number of Christians worked in the office with me.

Sherrie's voice broke through my dark thoughts one day. My co-worker stood next to me with a stack of manila folders, and when I finally realized she was there, I blushed. She had said my name a couple of times. "Hey, Saundra, are you okay?"

"Uh … sure. What did you need?"

"Well, actually, I wanted to invite you to go to a women's conference with me."

I knew that I stood at a crossroads in my life. *I need something to help me out of this dark place.*

I took down the details and made plans to go the following weekend.

As the date came closer, though, I couldn't find a babysitter. Packing Timothy with me, I made a special effort to go on Friday but had to leave early. On Saturday, I was able to return by myself.

I sat between Sherrie and Crystal, a woman my mother's age who I knew from The Life Center.

A woman of about 50 was introduced and came to the

podium to tell her story. She began to talk about her son. Her love of her children and pride at being a mother was evident. Her voice broke when she spoke of her son. "Drew was just a young adult, with his whole life ahead of him when he chose to end it. My Andrew committed suicide."

A hush swept across the crowd of a couple hundred women. There was silence and then sniffling could be heard throughout the group.

"Andrew believed that he would not be missed, that his life didn't matter." She paused to regain composure. "I miss him."

Her simple words sliced straight into my heart. I'd never seriously considered suicide, but I often felt as if my life was hopelessly ruined beyond repair, that my family would be better off without me and the embarrassment I'd brought.

Andrew's mother missed him. She saw the hidden treasure in him that God had created and apparently this young man never recognized.

*How could I think that I would not be missed? My parents, my sister, my husband, my children. Of course I matter to them. We matter to God even more than our children matter to us. Hadn't I returned to Kamiah and found acceptance and love in the church where I first accepted Jesus?*

Suddenly, I remembered the value that I had felt in my heart when I prayed with Pastor Bomley and my dad when I was only 5. A glimmer of hope reflected off of a presence inside of me. I remembered the feeling of having a gem placed there.

A new thought dawned on me: *God must have created me with some potential and purpose.*

When the woman finished speaking, Crystal reached over and took my hand. "Saundra, I pray for you every single day."

"Really?" The strange disclosure astounded me. "Is that a good thing or a bad thing?"

Teary-eyed, all three of us laughed. Crystal went on, "Jesus loves you very much."

"Can he forgive me even if I've done some really horrible things?" I asked.

"Yes," both of my friends answered emphatically.

"Not only has he forgiven you," Crystal continued gently, "but he has covered over those sins and taken them away. He will never hold them against you. Nor can anyone else."

I again prayed and asked forgiveness of my sins, so many it seemed that had piled up since I was 5. Yet I felt the same cleansing, the same transformation as I had before, now with a depth of understanding.

Crystal explained, "If you are reminded of the things that you've just confessed and given to the Lord, it is not the Lord dragging them out. That is the devil's doing. He wants to steal your faith and make you feel worthless."

I caught a glimpse of the treasure in my life when I returned to Kamiah and found that God's people loved and accepted me. Everywhere and everything to which I had looked had turned up empty until I turned back toward the place it all began.

But coming back home was not enough.

Often we bury the treasure that is in us by heaping unforgiveness upon ourselves. What God has forgiven in me, I cannot let the enemy dig up and dump back on me. And I mustn't throw dirt on top of the treasure myself.

With two truly accepting friends beside me, I surrendered to God. I rejected the lies I'd listened to all of my life and received the forgiving words of Jesus. "If we confess our sins, he is faithful and just and will forgive us our sins and cleanse us from all unrighteousness" (I John 1:9).

I've made mistakes since. I've experienced the accusations and the consequences and the temptations of my past. I'm in process.

I know that the truth sparkles within me, though. I've been permanently included in something very big and very wonderful. I'm accepted by the only one who really matters. God has adopted me into his family and into his heaven. I recognize his voice: "Saundra, I love you, and I have forgiven you."

Jesus Christ, the son of God, was the treasure I had been seeking all along.

# SURRENDER TO WIN
## THE STORY OF MARK YEARGIN
### WRITTEN BY ANGELA PRUSIA

"Want to have some real fun?" Steve held out a brown paper bag. A few years older than most of us at the party, he seemed to relish the attention in the center of our group.

"Whatcha got?" someone piped up.

"Samples." The bag crinkled as Steve pulled out a handful of prescription drugs. "My mom works in a doctor's office, so she gets free drugs."

Several loud whoops tore through the room. Hands of varying shades reached in the bag.

It was likely that Steve broke into the office and stole the drugs. I didn't care. I couldn't wait to get high. Six months earlier, I'd gotten my first high shooting up crystal meth, a hard drug with a potent punch. Most kids started their drug abuse by smoking pot, but not me: I jumped right into the deep end.

"Let's party!" I yelled, popping three blue morphine tablets into my mouth. I didn't know much about morphine except that it was a lot like heroin. I was excited about trying another "hard" drug.

Pieces of a Monopoly game lay scattered on a table, forgotten. Most of the partiers took speed, so they bounced off the walls while lethargy overtook me. My legs got heavy, and I collapsed behind the couch, out of sight from the others.

Tremors shook me, so I tried to brace myself against the couch, only to push my body further from view. Laughter surrounded me; panic seized me. Paralysis shut down my muscles. I couldn't scream for help; my vocal cords wouldn't move.

I stared at the ceiling, shaking and completely helpless.

Suddenly thick yellow-black smoke curled along the ceiling like demonic fingers. Long tendrils motioned me to follow its source. The tremors stopped, and I felt my spirit begin to rise from my body. Horror gripped me. I was dying, and hell awaited my arrival.

"Hey, Mark," a voice sounded in the distance. "What're you doing back there?" Hands grabbed my ankles and pulled me from certain death.

I couldn't answer. Slowly the smoke disappeared, and the hellish vision cleared.

"Get up, man." Steve, our party supplier, pulled me to my feet and helped me stand. "You don't look so good. We better get you walking."

I stumbled worse than a drunkard, but my muscles began to relax. Fear left.

Hell didn't scare me as much as death. If I died, I couldn't party. And I lived to party.

❧ ❧ ❧

A few weeks later, I hung out with a friend who'd

recently been in an accident. When I spied his bottle of pain pills, the temptation was too great. I took the bottle even though I'd never stolen from a friend before. A thought thrashed around my head, and I couldn't quit thinking about death.

That evening, I walked to the lake in our Florida neighborhood. I found a deserted dock and sat down on the still-warm planks. Water lapped against the edge as I swallowed the entire bottle of pills.

"This is it," I muttered into the growing darkness and lay down, already groggy.

The next thing I knew, someone shook my shoulder. I opened an eye, and sunlight made me squint.

"What're you doing?" my friend asked.

I sat up, feeling like a bear after hibernation. I'd never slept so well in my life.

"I don't know." I couldn't remember what had depressed me. I just wanted to sleep, so I headed for home.

Later, I piled into the trunk of a buddy's car with some other kids to sneak into the drive-in theater. I wanted to see the movie *Billy Jack*, but I could hardly stay awake.

I'd escaped death twice in one summer, and neither experience even fazed me.

☙☙☙

I hated high school. We moved across town, so I didn't know anyone. I was always a rebel. I wore my hair long when everyone kept it short and then cut it short when everyone wore it long. But now I didn't fit anywhere. I finally dropped out and enrolled at the vo-tech school for diesel mechanics to appease my parents. A friend there introduced me to a drug dealer.

"You want drugs?" he sneered. "Sell for me, and you'll get all the drugs you need."

I couldn't pass up an offer that good. The dealer was too old for the high school crowd, so I would be his front man.

I pretended to leave my parents' home every morning for the vo-tech school. In reality, I drove to the high school, slept in my car until break and sold drugs. I slept again until lunch and sold more drugs.

The set-up lasted about six months until my parents found out about the drugs. They tried to lay down the law, but I refused to obey.

"I'm leaving," I announced one night.

Mom teared up and disappeared into the back room. She wouldn't fight me; neither would Dad. They both hated conflict after growing up in homes with parents who constantly fought.

Dad gave me a lift to the interstate the next morning on his way to work. "I can't talk you out of this, can I?" He pulled over where I could hike down the embankment.

I answered by slamming the door and slung my pack over my shoulder. It carried only a few possessions.

"Good luck," he called out the open window without showing any emotion.

I waved and watched him take off, anticipation rising

within me. It was the 70s. Lots of kids hitchhiked around the country, and I couldn't wait to start my adventure.

∾ ∾ ∾

I hitchhiked from Orlando to the Keys, where I spent my nights sleeping on the beach and my days drinking and smoking pot. When I got hungry, I shoplifted for food. I found friends like me, including this girl Maddie and her boyfriend from Rhode Island.

The night before they left, I dreamed Maddie had died, and I saw her lying in an open casket. I couldn't shake the ominous feeling, so I decided to tag along.

Three days later, we ended up in Maddie's neighborhood, a rough area in the inner city of Providence. After her boyfriend headed home, we took a walk.

Soon an old black Cadillac pulled up alongside us. I knew something was up when a black Mercedes parked behind the Cadillac.

"You threw something at my ride!" This psycho jumped out and blocked our path. He reminded me of a bulldog.

"Nah, man." I shook my head. The guy was high or trying to start something. "We didn't do nothin'."

"You callin' me a liar?" He got all red.

We noticed a police car coming up the street, and it slowed as it approached.

"Here come the cops, Tony," this lady screamed from

the Caddy. Two kids peered out the back of the chauffeur-driven Mercedes, their faces pressed to the glass.

"I don't care," Tony yelled back. "I'll kill them, too!" The cops looked at Tony and pulled away, not wanting to get involved.

My heart hammered inside my throat. The dream that haunted me played out before my eyes. Maddie would die, and so would I.

"Hey, Tony," another voice called out. "What's up? You want to get something to eat?"

Tony cursed. "I gotta take care of a couple of losers." He edged closer to me. "This piece of trash threw something at my ride."

"No, no. They've been running around with me all night," the guy lied. It turned out he was a friend of Maddie's.

Tony backed down, but in a last show of bravado, he grabbed a grappling hook from the Cadillac. "Lucky for you losers," he sneered. "I was planning to hook each of you through the chest and throw you into the river."

I didn't doubt his threats. Later, Maddie's friend told me just how messed up Tony was. The guy killed people and brought along his wife and kids for entertainment. The kids watched from the safety of the black Mercedes.

I spent a couple nights on the floor of Maddie's living room before hitchhiking back to Orlando. I returned to life on the streets selling drugs. Escaping death was becoming my mantra.

# SURRENDER TO WIN

࿊ ࿊ ࿊

"You want to take her off my hands?" My buddy jumped out of a cream-colored VW bug. He'd stolen it from a dealership a few months earlier, and he was getting nervous.

Wheels sounded fun, so I spray-painted the bug a dull blue-gray and pulled off some chrome to make the car look worthless — hippies in a new bug looked suspicious, hippies in an old beater made sense. A few weeks later, I asked some North Carolina friends I'd met if they wanted to drive out west to a festival. We headed to Boulder, Colorado, pooling our money for gas and donating blood when we needed more cash.

The festival was basically a well-meaning gathering of hippies interested in communal living and brotherly love, not the drugs and sex most people associate with hippies. About five years earlier than Woodstock, innocence and naivety prevailed. Hiking back into the woods, I stopped along the trail for a breather and ended up talking with a guy who I noticed was missing part of a finger.

"Do you know who that was?" my friend asked when he met up with me almost an hour later.

I shook my head as we headed up the rest of the trail.

"Jerry Garcia from the Grateful Dead."

Later when I saw him playing guitar on TV, I saw his finger and remembered our visit.

At the gathering, my North Carolina friends introduced me to a pretty girl named Gail. Her Canadian accent and sweet way caught my attention. We hit it off and decided to get married so she could live in the country. Since she couldn't live in the States while she waited for her visa, we moved to Canada, and I applied for a social insurance card and worked for the city. I was 18; by 19, we were in the hospital, awaiting the birth of our first child.

"Gail, you've struggled for three days now," the doctor told us when he came into the labor room. "You need a C-section."

I looked at my wife, knowing the answer even before she refused. Gail wanted a natural childbirth, but I didn't want to see her suffer anymore. Several couples had come and gone home with new infants since our arrival.

"No!" Gail was adamant. "I don't want a C-section, I can do this." She believed surgery and pain medication made her a failure.

When the doctor couldn't convince Gail, he pulled me aside. "You're going to lose them both if you wait much longer. We only need your signature to operate."

I signed the papers and waited in an observation room used for student doctors. When the baby arrived, I was so worried our drug abuse might cause a birth defect that I immediately counted fingers and toes. When the nurse wrapped our baby in a blanket, I realized I didn't know the sex.

"Was it a girl or a boy?" I blurted out.

"A girl," the nurse laughed. "Good job, Dad. We all figured you'd pass out."

# SURRENDER TO WIN

❧❧❧

Becoming a father settled me down a little. I stayed away from hard drugs, but I continued to drink beer and smoke pot. I held minimum-wage jobs when I could, including work at two different sweatshops when my temporary visa expired and I became an illegal alien. Gail wasn't legal in the States yet, so we'd run the border on unguarded wintry back roads with a baby, a dog and little or no money.

When Gail finally received her visa, we moved back to Florida, and I took a construction job on a big Navy housing project in Jacksonville. Unfortunately, the extra money was too tempting. For five years, a steady supply and income cemented my addiction. My temper flared more and more. One time, I dumped our furniture outside and chopped it up like firewood. Another time, I almost beat a guy to death at a party.

A few weeks before the Navy housing contract ran out, a buddy and I decided we'd rather quit than get fired.

"This is bull!" I stormed into the supervisor's trailer and started cursing.

"You can't just lay us off after five years!" my buddy yelled.

We yelled some more and pelted the windows with rocks on our way out.

My buddy pulled out his pistol. *Bam!* We shot at the street lights to emphasize our point as we peeled out of the site.

# SINK OR SWIM

Out of habit the next morning, I came to work with only a vague memory of my outburst. Of course, I had no job.

❧❧❧

Things unraveled quickly. I found some work, but not enough to support my addiction, so Gail took our daughter and left. My parents let me move in, only to watch me overdose. I refused to go to the hospital, so they spent the night alternating between wrapping me in a blanket and bringing me ice water to drink. I shivered so badly that I bit into a hard plastic tumbler and broke it. At 6 feet, 2 inches and 145 pounds, I was a walking skeleton.

Gail and my daughter returned briefly, and we found a small house. Gail was as strung out as me, so events escalated even further.

With rent due and no groceries, I got desperate one night. Since I'd worked a little in the food industry, I knew the typical nightshift routine. Employees cleaned up while the manager counted the cash drawers. I figured I could slip in the back door when someone came outside to empty the trash.

Everything went according to plan except for my nerves. I snuck in the back, pulled out my gun and demanded money. I was more of a wreck than the employees. I grabbed a handful of cash and spilled half of it before I dashed out of the building. Back home, I didn't even have enough for a fourth of the rent, so I got high.

# SURRENDER TO WIN

The police came banging on my door a few days later with a search warrant, no doubt alerted by Gail, who was mad that we still had no groceries or rent.

"Get your hands in the air," one of them demanded, while the others circled around me like I was some kind of rabid animal.

"Daddy!" my daughter, Sandy, wailed from a corner of the room. She couldn't understand what was happening to me. She was too young to see the monster everyone else knew.

I held my hands up and paced in a circle. The drugs made me feel invincible. No way was I going to jail. If I could knock out the biggest guy, I could handle the smaller two near the back door. I sucker-punched my target and watched his head pop back like a toy I had as a kid called "Rock 'Em Sock 'Em Robots." I spun around, only to get hit on the back of the head with the barrel of a pistol. The biggest guy tackled me with fury. He wrapped his arm under my chin, choking me so bad, I thought I'd die.

"Hands behind your back!" Facedown, wedged into the recliner, my hands were pinned.

"No," Sandy wailed. "Don't hurt my daddy."

The big cop glanced at my daughter and softened. Later, I learned if it weren't for Sandy, he would've shot me in the middle of my living room. If I'd been a cat, I'd have used more than my nine lives by now.

"Hands behind your back!" The big cop pressed me harder.

# SINK OR SWIM

When he realized I wasn't fighting, but stuck, he loosened his grip. "I'll let you breathe, but you gotta cooperate."

"There's a pistol in his boot," Gail told them, standing calmly off to the side as if relieved life with me was finally over. They handcuffed me and shoved me out the door.

Multiple charges faced me: armed robbery, assault of an officer, concealed weapon, illegal weapon because I had a sawed off 12-gauge in my house and possession of drugs and drug paraphernalia. The detectives said I was looking at 30 years to life.

ॐॐॐ

I sized up the judge, a thin man with dark hair. He'd just given the guy before me another 10 years for a sarcastic comment, and his only charge was heroin possession. The public defender's earlier words rang in my ears: *Plead guilty to the robbery, and the other charges will be dropped. You'll be in prison for 15 to 30 years.*

"Your Honor," I started. "I'm so sorry. Robbing the restaurant was stupid and irresponsible." My mother sniffled behind me, and I heard my dad reach his arm around her. "I have a drug problem, and I need help, not prison."

I babbled on another five minutes before the judge stopped me. Irritation clouded his face. I didn't have a chance.

"Enough." The judge wrote something and shuffled

the papers in front of him. "Five years at the Florida State Prison. Next!"

I should've been grateful, but now the reality of prison time hit me, and I whined to the bailiff.

He shook his head. "The judge sentenced you to 15 years before he even saw you. Add to that, Florida's three-year minimum mandatory sentencing requirement for felonies with a firearm, and you're one lucky Joe. I can't figure out why you got off so easy."

God rescued me again. But I wasn't just blind; I was stupid.

৵৵৵

Nineteen months later, I walked out of prison on parole and filed for divorce. The chip on my shoulder grew. My only remorse came from getting caught. My sister had adopted Sandy a year earlier since both Gail and I were unfit parents. I slipped into the convict's dream, working enough to satisfy parole conditions while stealing and dealing on the side. *Nice guys finish last, right?*

Getting high wasn't fun anymore, just necessary. I lost interest in living. Nothing felt good; nothing felt bad. Everything simply felt … empty.

I married a girl I met at a bar who was just as messed up as me. Somehow, I figured getting married would magically make things turn around. The divorce was finalized 10 months later. In a feeble attempt to save the marriage, I enrolled in a 28-day treatment program.

# SINK OR SWIM

A friend picked me up the last day of treatment, and I got high before we even left the parking lot. I became a mule, hauling drugs from Florida to Pennsylvania, living in motels when I could afford it; when I couldn't, I slept in a car the bank was trying to repossess. Life didn't change until Memorial Day 1987.

☙☙☙

I woke up groggy, behind my steering wheel taking in the surroundings, and noticed I was parked outside the emergency room entrance at the hospital.

*What was I doing here?* I wasn't injured. *Had I brought someone for help?* I racked my brain, searching for details, but nothing came. I had a pistol in my pocket, but it hadn't been fired. Panic seized me. My last memory was drinking and trying to sell the last of my pot three days earlier. I'd blacked out before, but never this long.

Worse, I'd just seen an HBO special about people on death row who couldn't remember the crimes they'd committed while in a blackout. I'd already spent time in prison; I didn't want to go back. I wasn't any better than those inmates facing death.

For the first time in my life, I realized the magnitude of my problem. I needed help. I whipped out of the parking lot and headed to the only person who'd kept clean after rehab, an outgoing guy named Ray who'd lost a leg from a bone disease.

"I need help," I confessed to Ray.

# SURRENDER TO WIN

He looked me in the eye. "If you want to get clean and stay clean, I'll rent you my garage as a bedroom. You have to come with me to AA every night."

I agreed; I could always play along until I got back on my feet, then I'd take off on another "run."

My plans never seemed to work out like I thought they would.

☙☙☙

God got a hold of me through Alcoholics Anonymous. I listened to people talk about going through things like I'd been through, and they were getting better. They would pray at the beginning and end of the meeting. I started to feel better; I went back to work. Before I knew it, I'd been clean 30 days, 60 days, 90 days, then six months and a year.

The founders of AA had the wisdom to recognize they would turn people away if they tried to force God on alcoholics and addicts. First the abuse has to stop, then the praying starts and before you know it, God has revealed himself and the relationship has been restored. I met God early on, but I started on baby food. One step at a time, one day at a time.

Surrender is everything. I could accept that my addictions were a much greater power than myself. So it wasn't much to recognize I needed to depend on a power greater than myself to stop the problem. When I finally surrendered, an incredible pressure lifted from me.

# SINK OR SWIM

For about the first five years, I went to AA and Narcotics Anonymous meetings seven days a week. As the years passed, my meeting attendance declined, but my relationship with God grew. In and out of the meetings, I prayed the Serenity Prayer:

*God grant me the serenity*
*to accept the things I cannot change,*
*courage to change the things I can*
*and wisdom to know the difference.*

It took me longer before I could pray the Lord's Prayer. I couldn't get past how much I'd screwed up. *How can I ask God for anything when I've done nothing but disappoint him?*

Knowing how many times he'd spared me from death, I could only thank him each morning for saving me. Gratitude changed my perspective. Over the years, my prayers grew as God revealed himself to me, and I began to understand Love who would die in my place.

❧❧❧

Amazingly, God began to restore my relationship with my daughter and the rest of my family. I married a recovering alcoholic named Dawn, and we've been together now for 20 years. A neck injury prevented me from working construction any longer, so I went to school to become an appraiser, a job I really enjoy. I've been clean nearly 23 years and have sponsored several people who've broken their addictions. Only those who surrender to God find success.

In 1994, I received a full pardon from Florida governor Lawton Chiles and his cabinet. Far more amazing is the pardon I received from God. Unlike the governor's pardon, everyone who asks Jesus to pardon him or her receives total forgiveness. The slate is wiped clean.

I get a kick out of the old bumper sticker that reads "God is my co-pilot." God is my pilot. On a good day, I may be a co-pilot, but usually, I'm just a passenger. I know I have no business running my own life — all my best thinking only led to overdoses, attempted suicide, prison, divorce, addiction and pain. Joy and purpose came when I finally surrendered to God.

Dawn and I moved to Idaho in 2003 when we got tired of the crowds in Florida. When we visited The Life Center in 2008, we knew we'd found home. In addition to being a part of two life groups, I've enjoyed driving the van on Wednesday nights to bring kids to youth group.

"Hey there," I greet each one as they get on the bus. The first kid on the bus will usually talk to me until we pick up another kid and it becomes uncool to talk to an adult.

I smile, remembering myself at the same age. If only I'd found a youth group and learned how to have a relationship with a God worthy of surrender.

"Have fun!" I call out as they head up the steps and clamor into the youth room.

# SINK OR SWIM

I pray every day that these kids won't stray down the same path I followed. "Help them, God. They need you."

I can almost hear an audible voice. "Trust me, Mark. Remember I never left you."

"Search me, O God, and know my heart;
test me and know my anxious thoughts.
See if there is any offensive way in me, and lead me
in the way everlasting." (Psalm 139:23-24)

# CHERISHED HEART
## THE STORY OF ETHEL BOMLEY
### WRITTEN BY ARLENE SHOWALTER

"No longer will they call you Deserted,
or name your land Desolate. But you will be called
Hephzibah, and your land Beulah; for the
LORD will take delight in you …" (Isaiah 62:4)

"I'll kill you if you tell. I swear I will." The drawn-back fist that had so often imprinted my face and soul loomed before my eyes. I believed her.

After seven endless years of threats, punches and assertions of worthlessness, deliverance came in the form of a praying treasure named Aunt Pearl.

### Battered Heart

My world shattered when I was 3 years old.

"Where's my daddy? Why doesn't Daddy come home?"

Silence.

"Is he mad at me?"

Silence. Nobody offered comfort or explanation for Daddy's sudden disappearance. That vacuum of unanswered questions remained in my heart for more than 40 years.

# SINK OR SWIM

My mother fell ill.

"Let me take Ethel until you get on your feet," Pastor Ethel, whom I'd been named after, offered. Mama jumped at the offer. She also farmed out my older brother, Dustin, to live with our aunt and uncle.

Only my half-sister, Glenda, 16 years my senior, remained with her. The two forged a formidable team that overshadowed my young life.

"Come to Essie Mama," my guardian crooned, her blue eyes glowing. "I have a surprise for you."

I ran to Pastor Ethel, throwing myself into her welcoming arms. She bore me to the garage and flung the door open. Its resounding thwack echoed the thump of my heart. There stood the most perfect-in-the-world darling playhouse, just for me.

I jumped down and dashed to it. Snookie, her German shepherd dog, barked his approval, bouncing about like a released spring. He followed me into the playhouse, tail thwapping against its petite walls, as I oohed and ahhed over every perfect item.

"Now, don't you bite her," Essie Mama often lectured him.

"And don't you tease him," she'd instruct me.

Only once I pushed the longsuffering pooch too far. He snatched my hand with the tender mouth of a bird dog, holding it lightly and unharmed between his teeth. After a hurried conference, we consented together to keep that little secret from Essie Mama.

"Essie Mama's very sick," my mother informed me

after three years of perfect, harmonious bliss. "She has double pneumonia. You can stay with Glenda and me until she gets better."

Then I got sick. Flirting-with-death sick. Glenda and Mama came and went. I saw their blurred sad faces through fevered eyes. I heard whispered conferences. As slow as a loaded sleigh pulled without snow, I recovered.

"Ethel." Mama cleared her throat. She and Glenda exchanged pinched glances. "We have something to tell you."

I drew my covers tight against my chin and waited.

"Essie Mama went to be with Jesus."

Mute tears rolled down my cheeks, dripping onto the blanket I clutched.

"When you get better, we'll all move to St. Joseph. I have family there."

They left.

My throat closed against choking sobs.

No hugs.

No kisses.

No condolences.

I cried my 6-year-old heart dry.

We moved. I reveled in sharing a home with Mama again.

Three happy months passed in a blink, then Mama got sick.

"Ethel." Her weakened voice summoned me to her room. "I need to talk to you."

I sat down next to her bed.

"I can't take care of you," she began. "Essie Mama's sister, Irene, has offered to take you in." Coughing slowed her explanation. "She can't have children of her own and feels this is God's call on her life. She and her husband can give you more than I ever could."

I blinked away tears as my heart thumped in disappointment. The next day, I pressed my face against the window as Mama's and Glenda's faces retreated from the moving car. Nobody bothered to ask what *I* wanted.

My first six months with Irene and Pete were as good as could be to a lonely 7 year old who preferred to be home with her own family. They lived in a beautiful house, fed me well and bought me nice clothes. Mama beamed every time she saw me.

She pursued other interests with a light heart, knowing she had given her daughter a better life. She started a mission in a store front, which remained open for more than 20 years.

ॐॐॐ

"I'll kill you!" Irene shrieked.

I dashed from the kitchen on hunted-deer feet. Fleet, but not fleet enough. She grabbed my arm, flinging me into a nearby chair. Lightning fists beat a vicious tattoo on my face, accompanied by thunderous screams.

The doorbell rang.

*Rescued!*

My heart soared.

# CHERISHED HEART

"Get in that bathroom, and clean yourself up," she hissed, chewing each word and spitting it like used tobacco in my face. Then she lowered her voice to death volume. "You say one word … I'll kill you." The hellish glow in her eyes affirmed her intent.

I obeyed with the quiet surrender of the condemned.

Mama entered the house, innocent of the event, and left the same way. I excelled at the only control I possessed — over my emotions.

Irene's husband, Pete, worked as a chef. He left the house in the early afternoon, not returning until early morning. He seldom witnessed the abuse. But when he did, he stood up for me.

"Take that girl back to her mother," he bellowed.

"Shut up and mind your own business," she flung back.

They fought.

Irene won.

I stayed — and lost.

Pete provided the only sliver of joy in those dreadful years. Every Saturday he took me grocery shopping, buying all the food for the next week. He instructed the butcher exactly how to cut and trim each piece of meat.

"Here, Ethel," he said, before we reached the house. He slipped a silver dollar into my small hand. "This is for you. Save it for Christmas." Irene deleted Christmas from her household.

"You stupid clod!" Irene snatched up a butcher knife, brandishing it like death's messenger, when I dropped the salt shaker. It crashed to the immaculate floor I'd scrubbed. "Get in the basement before I kill you."

I ran to the door, prepared to spend terrified basement time in the dark — a now too-familiar routine. But this time, she seized my arm and flung me down the steps.

"Nobody loves you," she shrieked from her lofty stance at the top. "Nobody wants you. How could anyone love your ugly face?"

With shaking fingers, I traced a faint scar between my nose and lips. I had been born with a cleft lip, which required surgery two days after my birth and again when I was 3. My father disappeared shortly after the second surgery. *Was it my fault Daddy left? Did Daddy think I was ugly? Does Mama? Is that why she keeps giving me away like an unwanted pet?* I huddled on the cold, unfeeling concrete, leaning forward to rest my anguished brow on the bottom riser. Alone and unloved — a solitary discard of life.

The insatiable furnace roared a few feet away. Already, it had devoured every toy I owned — every doll I prized. Irene fed them into it, and it responded with fiery delight.

Once, while Irene worked in the laundry area, she spotted a mouse meandering about the basement. With a hellish grin, she picked up a piece of stovepipe and crept upon it with catlike grace.

*Wham!* She had the mouse captured.

She lifted the stovepipe just enough for the mouse to partially escape, then brought it down again with a bang.

The mouse squealed.

Over and over she repeated this process, slowly skinning the screaming mouse alive.

And, like a cat, she tired of the sport once her prey had perished. She picked up flayed remains, tossing them into the same furnace that had gobbled up all my lovely things.

"You'll get the same if you ever tell," she threatened.

I experienced my first menstrual cycle at age 12, clueless as to what was going on with my body. Irene and I were visiting some of her friends when the second one came. Trying not to show pain, I excused myself when terrible cramps hit. Once in the bathroom, I discovered my panties had filled with blood and seeped through to the seat of my dress.

Irene hurried me from the house when she took note of my stained skirt. "You stupid clod!" she ranted all the way to a nearby drugstore. She dragged me to the appropriate aisle, then to the checkout, punctuating every hostile step with an angry barrage.

"Twirl around, dummy," she ordered as she pulled a wallet from her Italian leather handbag. "Let everyone get a good look at your stupidity."

I obeyed. I always obeyed.

She shoved me through the door when we got to her house. "Get in the bathroom, and clean yourself up."

### *Hopeful Heart*

*Ring. Ring.*
Even at 14, I knew better than to answer the phone.

In three steps, Irene had snatched up the receiver and purred into it. "Hello?"

Her commanding face bled white, then red, then purple. Then with one deliberate flip of her wrist, she dropped it into its cradle.

A silent cloud pervaded her countenance like released mustard gas in the Great War.

"Get in the car."

The silence engulfed me as completely as the fulminating ash of Mt. St. Helens. She offered no explanations. Fear kept my trembling lips sealed.

Soon we pulled up in front of my mother's mission, where she lived in a back room. Irene hurried me through the door and into Mama's apartment. My petite aunt, Pearl, sat nearby. Tight faces greeted us.

"Sit," Mama commanded.

We sat.

I stared at my knees, willing them not to knock together. *Why has Mama called us over? Why do she and Aunt Pearl look so upset?*

"I understand you have been abusing my daughter." Mama addressed Irene. The quiet accusation hung in the air like a pregnant thundercloud.

Irene leapt from her seat, charged at my mother and grabbed her clothes. She raised that all-too-familiar fist and aimed for Mama's face.

Aunt Pearl rose, stepping quickly to Mama. The power of God fell like a lightning bolt, sending Irene across the room. She flopped onto the couch with arms upraised and mouth agape, pinned by God, frozen and speechless.

"The Lord told me in prayer what you have been doing to Ethel," Aunt Pearl stated. She laid out facts that only God, Irene and I knew.

Irene sat helpless, agape and hands raised in surrender, until Aunt Pearl turned to sit next to her sister. Only then did God release her. She lowered her arms, shaking her head. Then she jumped to her feet.

"I tried to help you," she shrieked. "This is the thanks I get. Your mission will close for this," she threatened, snatching up her purse to leave.

"Don't come back," Mama retorted.

"You'll be fine now, Ethel," Aunt Pearl told me. Her eyes twinkled. "The Lord is watching out for you."

The mission prospered in spite of Irene's threats. But the thoughts of Irene's threats held me in an iron grip. I jumped every time the phone rang. I checked the sidewalks, both ways, every time I left the house. Her words haunted me, coating my heart with clammy fear.

Despite my fears, however, colossal joy engulfed my heart. Mama and me — together at last! Every time she passed me, I longed to express my gladness with hugs. I longed to be held by her.

"Don't, Ethel." Mama pushed me away with an impatient hand. "This is not the time for hugs."

I needed glasses and selected frames with great care.

"How do I look?" I turned to my mother. A small frown creased her brow.

"Those would look better on Glenda."

# SINK OR SWIM

I sang with my whole being at services.

"Glenda sings better."

❧ ❧ ❧

I sat as close as I dared to my boyfriend in the theater, feeling quite grown up at 15 — even though two friends and their dates watched the movie with us. I enjoyed it until the scene showing a young girl washed overboard.

Rescuers found and covered her body with a tarp. One limp hand remained exposed, limp and lifeless.

I felt the Holy Spirit whisper into my spirit, *If that had been you, where would you be now?*

Fear gripped me. I had just recovered from pneumonia. I didn't know Jesus and knew if I had died, I would be without him forever. I spurted from my seat, urgency propelling me to the nearest exit. My boyfriend followed in my desperate wake.

"What's wrong?" he gasped. "Did I offend you?"

"It has nothing to do with you." I threw the words over my shoulder. "I just have to get home right now. Go back and finish the movie."

He finally recognized my determination, turned and went back to the theater.

I continued my mad dash home, bursting through the door, drenched from the pouring rain. Glenda took one look at me and wrapped her housecoat about my shivering body. She took a towel and wrapped it about my head.

"Ethel, do you want to give your heart to the Lord?"

# CHERISHED HEART

An unfamiliar tenderness crept into a voice usually employed in complaints about her pesky younger sister.

"Yes," I cried. "Yes, yes, yes."

She steered me to the altar at our mother's mission with a gentle arm draped about my shoulders. I collapsed to my knees, pouring out my tortured heart to the Lord.

"Jesus," I cried, "I know I am unworthy of your grace, but please be merciful to me. Come into my heart, and forgive me of my many sins."

In that moment, I felt the Holy Spirit wash over my soul. I knew my prayer was answered.

*Irene lied to you,* Jesus whispered into my spirit. *She said you were no good and unworthy of love. She lied. You are good because I created you and I love you.*

As Jesus spoke, the Holy Spirit erased all the negative feelings Irene had thrust into me, leaving me in the blood of Jesus.

"Thank you, Jesus. Thank you," I cried, trembling now in joy. As praise flowed from my lips, new melodious sounds sprang forth. As waters rushing to the precipice, the melody rushed and tumbled, eager to reach their destination. God had instantaneously granted me his love language.

I knelt at the altar, soaking in total approval — complete acceptance for the first time in my life.

A liberated Ethel skipped off to school, eager to share her newfound friend, Jesus, with her classmates. Most laughed. Undeterred, I pressed on.

By 16, both Mama and Glenda felt I had all the

education I needed to get along in life, so they talked me out of going to school and into taking a job. I continued to share my love of Jesus everywhere I worked. I wanted everyone to know him.

One day, while I cleared and wiped down the lunch counter where I worked, I glanced up. A familiar figure strode toward me, arms swinging, swinging. Irene.

I stood my full height. Fear of my former tormentor had evaporated the night I met Jesus. Something rose up in me. Strength and a revelation.

*I am not under your power any longer. You will never intimidate me, frighten me or abuse me again.*

Our eyes met and locked. *I could knock you to kingdom come, if I wanted to.*

She stopped dead in her tracks, spun around on her heel and left the store. I never saw her again.

❧❧❧

I became an ordained minister at age 21, following the footsteps of my mother and Glenda. Often, my sister and I ministered together in preaching and song.

One night as we sang at another church in town, people flocked to the front during the altar call. Among them was a girl named Juanita. We became friends.

After Juanita's pastor and family left that church, she began attending my mother's mission. We had since moved from the back room to a two-story house in St. Joseph.

# CHERISHED HEART

Juanita, or Nita, as we called her, began hanging around our home to escape a difficult home environment.

"How would you like to live here with Ethel and me?" Mama asked her.

"Could I, Sister Short?" Nita's eyes mirrored amazement.

"Of course you can. Ethel would love it, too."

So, Nita came to live with us. At first, I enjoyed having my friend around all the time.

"Good morning, Nita." Mama greeted her with a warm hug and hot coffee.

"Good morning, Sister Short." A beaming Nita returned the hug while accepting the beverage.

"Good morning, Mama." I skipped into the kitchen on feet feathered in hope.

*This time she'll hug me, too.*

Mama stiffened at my touch. Her coffee sloshed on the table. "Be careful," she admonished, pushing my arm away. "Can't you do anything right?"

That afternoon, I found enough courage to confront her.

"You treat Nita better than you do me. You give her lots of attention, encouragement and compliments. I'm your flesh-and-blood daughter, but I'm treated like a street person." I blinked back the tears that blurred her impassive face. "Why?"

"You're making mountains out of molehills, Ethel." She waved a dismissive hand. "You make me nervous. Stop being so petty and grow up."

# SINK OR SWIM

## *Determined Heart*

Life had toughened me. I always finished what I started — no matter what. At 19, I was leading the last song of the service when a sudden pain clobbered me. *Gotta finish this song.*

I slogged on as the pain worsened, placing my hand over my chest. *Thump. Thump. Thump.*

*I must finish this song. I always finish what I start.* Perspiration beaded across my forehead.

*Thump. Finish the song.* Last verse. *I can make it … I can.* The last note echoed and ended. I sat down, screened by the pulpit, gasping for pain-free breath. I staggered to my feet and into the back room.

I lay down and did the only thing available to me — I prayed.

*Lord, I don't know what is wrong with me, but I need your help.*

Instantly the pain lifted. I knew he healed me. He lulled me into confident slumber.

"Ethel." Nita touched my shoulder. "You promised to go apartment hunting with me today."

Although I knew Jesus healed me, I felt very weak. But my word was my word. I got up and followed Nita out the door.

I didn't tell her about the incident. Or Mama. Or Glenda. Only Jesus knew my secret.

❧❧❧

# CHERISHED HEART

A year later, Glenda, her husband and I returned from ministering at a youth revival in Kansas. My body and soul ached with weariness.

"I'm going upstairs for a nap," I said.

I threw my body across the bed, weighted with sorrow. I had just broken off a relationship with a good man because I knew he wasn't the right one for me.

*Oh, Lord, it breaks my heart that I had to break his heart. I want a home and family of my own. All my friends are married. What do you want for my life?*

Pain pierced my chest with the swiftness of a well-aimed arrow. I felt myself leave my body and float to the ceiling. Wind blew through an open window, tickling the curtains with warm summer air. I floated through the ceiling and onto the roof.

I heard a lawnmower humming below. I sniffed the crisp, clean odor. My senses  heightened. The blue sky deepened to heavenly intensity. Kids played below, their carefree laughter teasing my ears.

I looked up. Before me lay a path stretching upward into heaven. I stepped onto it, placing one foot before the other. Twilight bathed me in hushed comfort. I walked on.

Then I saw a bright light approaching. *Jesus!* He held his arms wide in wordless invitation. I ran to him — straight into his arms. He embraced me with the same loving fierceness of a father receiving his rescued child from the arms of a soot-covered fireman.

*Total love ... absolute acceptance ... infinite peace.*

Then he reached up and took my hands from his neck.

"Come. I have some things to show you."

We strolled forward, hand in hand, through a beautiful countryside, but I saw little. I kept my eyes on him. Only him.

We approached a group of people, bent over as if working the ground. The moment they caught sight of Jesus, they straightened up. Brilliant smiles lit every face as they opened their mouths to praise him.

Their joy encompassed us. He radiated his own joy. Joys mingled and meshed into a throbbing epic of delight.

"Look among the people, Ethel."

I looked. There stood Pastor Essie Mama and other folk from her church who'd passed on. I drank in their lustrous faces.

"Time to go." With loving firmness, he took my hand and led me on. We strolled by a tree-lined river. Flowers abounded, clothed in heaven's intensity. I saw other images, even beautiful mansions. But my eyes saw Jesus — only Jesus. Nothing and no one distracted me from his lovely face.

I wanted to stop and savor this time with him. I wanted to pick these vibrant, abundant flowers and drink in their scent — his scent. I wanted to lay down in the greener-than-green grass by the clear flowing river.

"No, Ethel. We must go on."

We moved on. I felt no disappointment because I traveled with him. He was everything to me. He filled my senses, blocking out all else.

He stopped and turned me to him. "I brought you here

to see these things," he explained, "for a purpose. But now I want you to go back."

In that instant, I remembered earth, which I'd forgotten in the thrill of his presence.

"You pierce my heart," I cried. "I don't want to go back. Please don't make me go back."

"You have to go back so I can fulfill what you asked for — a husband and children. And whenever I make a promise, it will happen as I said. You will also have a ministry. You have much to do and many places to go. Remember, *it will happen just as I said.*"

"No!" my anguished heart cried.

"You must go," he said with great kindness. "You must do these things I promised. I want you to tell everybody that I love them. You must tell them that I have prepared this beautiful place for them to be with me forever. I want them to love me and come to me. I can give them a beautiful life."

My reluctant feet found the path. Jesus helped with a little push earthward. I emerged from the blue sky. The sun still shone. The children played. The fresh-cut grass tickled my nostrils. I entered the room and saw my prone body lying where I'd left it — the one that suffered recurring back pain, due to abuse at Irene's hands.

"Must I return to this body?"

"Yes. You must fulfill what I showed you."

I obeyed, releasing a long, slow breath. I slept.

"Ethel, wake up." I shook my head and looked up. Mama stood over me, shaking my shoulder.

"Dinner's ready."

"I'm up."

She moved to the top of the stairs, then lifted an arm as though shielding her eyes.

"What happened to you?" she asked. "There is a bright glow all about you."

"I'll tell you in a minute." I reached for my hairbrush, ran it through my hair and then went down to the living room.

I sat across from Mama, recounting the story. She began weeping.

"To think I might have come upstairs and found you dead!"

∂∂∂

I ran to answer my ringing phone.

"Hi, Ethel, Valita here. Our church is having a youth rally tomorrow night. Will you go with me?"

"I don't see how I can," I replied. "We're in the middle of inventory at work."

"Please?" she asked. "Pastor Sherwood needs a piano player and asked me to ask you." She paused. "It would be quite appreciated. I'll come by and get you."

Seeing no gracious way out, I agreed.

Unbeknownst to me, Brother Sherwood and another pastor, Brother Silas Garret, had a plan to get a certain young man and me to meet.

As soon as Valita, her boyfriend and I entered the

church, I started for the front so I could warm up on the piano. Pastor Silas, sitting in a back pew, put out his hand and snagged mine.

"Sister Ethel," he said, drawing me to his seat with a smile. "I have someone I want you to meet." He and a handsome stranger rose to greet me.

"Ethel, Eldon Bomley. Eldon, Ethel Short."

"Nice to meet you." We shook hands, and I resumed my journey to the piano. Moments later, Eldon materialized beside me as I ran through a few chords.

"Pastor Silas asked me to sing a solo. Would you accompany me?"

"Of course."

I played.

Eldon beamed.

"May I drive you home?" he asked.

"No, thank you. I have a ride."

"Then, could I have your phone number?"

"Okay."

Valita briefed me on the ride home. "Eldon's a widower. His wife got sick on a Monday and died four days later. She left him with three kids." She paused. "That was four years ago. He's a good man, Ethel."

The "good man" called a few days later.

"Hello. This is Eldon. Could I take you out?"

"No. We're doing inventory at the store. I don't have time."

Eldon called again.

"Can I take you out?"

"No."

"Well, would you let me accompany you to your own services at the mission?"

"Okay."

My unassuming Prince Charming rolled up to our front door in a pickup truck.

"I farm 240 acres," he said with a laugh and a wave.

When Eldon brought me home, he turned off the motor, gripping the steering wheel hard.

"I hate to spoil a perfectly wonderful evening, but I have to be honest with you. I have three children. My wife died …"

"I know," I interrupted.

His beautiful brown eyes, like a startled buck's, stared at me.

"How in the world did you know?"

"My friend told me."

"Oh." Silence, then, "Ah … would you go out with me again?"

"Yes."

His eyes widened further.

"You will?"

"Yes."

He shook his befuddled head. "Every other girl says no as soon as I tell her I have kids."

Eldon arranged to take me to dinner to meet his young brood. After the hostess seated us, he cleared his throat.

"Ah … do you know anyone at this restaurant?"

"No," I answered, a bit bemused. "Why do you ask?"

# CHERISHED HEART

"I … um …" He stopped to study his placemat, as if searching for help. "I thought it might be a bit awkward for you to be here with me … and the kids."

"Are you uncomfortable?" I asked.

"Not if you're not."

"I'm not."

Relief flooded his handsome face.

I felt a prickle of love.

My forthrightness emboldened Eldon.

"Will you marry me?"

"I will."

"You don't have a strong heart," Mama pointed out when I displayed Eldon's ring on my finger. "And you're only 21. How do you expect to take on a husband and three children?"

I sent the ring back. "I can't marry you."

Eldon pleaded.

I acquiesced, and he returned the ring to me.

"The children will hamper your ministry," church elders intoned. "Mustn't be God's will."

"I can't marry you. Here's your ring."

I wanted God's will.

I fasted and prayed.

I cried.

"Will you marry me?"

"Yes."

"How can you adjust to farm living after living all your life in cities?"

"I can't marry you." More tears. The ring made its

third trip to Eldon's pocket. "Please do not write or call me ever again."

More fasting. More prayer. More tears.

I stopped talking, lost weight, withdrew.

"I don't know what's wrong with me," I cried, bursting into our kitchen where my mother and two friends sat visiting.

"You're in love, dummy," Mama said dryly. "Sit down. I have something important to tell you."

I sat.

"The Lord showed me during prayer that if you don't marry Eldon, you'll die of a broken heart. Marry him."

I jumped up, snagged the phone, dialed his number and waited.

"Hello."

"Hi, Eldon. What are you doing right now?"

"Coming over to see you."

"I thought I told you not to come around any longer. Remember?"

"Doesn't matter. I'm coming anyhow."

An hour later, the doorbell rang.

I stood rooted to the kitchen floor.

I glanced at our guests. "If you've ever prayed for me before, pray *now*."

"Oh, God, help her now," they echoed.

Somehow I made it as far as the living room before stopping. I looked at Eldon, standing in the front doorway. Eldon looked at me, standing in the living room doorway.

# CHERISHED HEART

*Lord, what can I say to this dear man whom I've turned down three times already?*

Eldon smiled. The sun came out. He opened his arms — wide. I ran into them. Safe, sheltering, loving, forgiving, accepting arms. Our tears met and melded.

"Will you marry me, Ethel?"

"Yes, and *nobody* will come between us again."

Eldon extended the ring. This time it stayed on my finger. Glenda married us at our mother's mission on a Tuesday night — almost three months to the day after we'd first met.

ৰুৰুৰু

That winter, Eldon hooked a sled to his tractor to pull the children and me through the snow. The wind exhilarated me. Children who loved and accepted me as their real mother surrounded me. Love filled my heart. Love — and excruciating pain.

"What's wrong?" Eldon caught sight of my pinched face.

"Heart," I breathed through tight lips.

Eldon helped me to the house. He laid hands on me and turned to God.

"Lord," he began, "heal your daughter. Heal her now in your son's gracious name. Amen."

The pain lifted. I got up to fix dinner for my family.

Thrice the enemy tried to take me out before my 22nd birthday. Thrice he failed.

# SINK OR SWIM

God began nudging Eldon's heart, calling him into full-time ministry. He listened and obeyed. On June 24, 1960, he received full ordination. Over the next years, we served together as pastors in Kansas, Iowa, Montana and Idaho.

Because of the abuse I'd suffered as a child, compassion flowed through me for the underdog, the unloved and the castoffs of earth.

As a young teen, I had gone into taverns, searching for and finding children for Sunday school. I scoured our neighborhood for needy children. I fed them, cleaned them up and taught them the love of Jesus.

Early in our ministry, Eldon and I ministered on the Crow reservation. We involved our children, who helped us tend to the sick. They changed their beds and cleaned their homes.

## Healing Heart

Life pushed on, busy and filled with joy. But God knew that deep in my heart hurts and issues lay entrenched which had never been exposed. He wanted complete healing.

My mother and I sat in a rare moment of quiet harmony in 1978. She was in her 78th year. I felt an unusual boldness come over me.

"Mama, do you mind if I ask you something?"

"Of course not. What is it?"

I searched for the right words, twisting my empty hands together.

"Why did you give me to Irene?"

Tears sprang into her eyes. She laid her hand on my arm.

"Irene's friend, Flo, just left my house," she began. Her voice quavered. "She told me everything that happened to you."

My heart lightened. *Now we can discuss the dark secrets of the past, bring them to the light and be done with them.* I bent toward her, eyes glowing, waiting for her next words.

"Honey, we won't talk about this anymore."

My heart plummeted, but I saw how weak she was. I knew she couldn't handle the truth. I couldn't upset her.

I buried my hopes in the depths, beside the old hurts. Mama died two years later.

છ્ર છ્ર છ્ર

Several other relatives died around the same time as Mama. Then our youngest child married and left home. A deep depression descended upon me.

But, true to the standards I had set early in life, I always finished what I started. I told nobody of my pain, not even my Eldon. I didn't want to burden him, and I thought he wouldn't understand anyway.

I continued to teach Sunday school and women's

retreats. I continued to read and pray, preach, write lessons. I stayed busy but grew desperate.

One day, during a ladies meeting, the leader stood to dismiss us.

"I'm sorry, sisters, but I can't release you yet. The Lord told me one of you in this room is hurting very badly and is in need of prayer."

She waited. Nobody moved.

*You know she's talking about you*, the Holy Spirit whispered.

*I can't go up there in front of all these women. They all know me. What will they think of me if they know I'm the one falling apart?*

"We will not leave until this sister receives prayer," the leader insisted.

Finally, the Lord lifted me from the seat. I hastened to the front. She opened her arms wide to accept me as I ran sobbing into them.

This lady knew nothing of my past, but she knew how to listen to God. As she prayed over me, she took my hands and peered deep into my eyes.

"I am taking the place of your mother," she said. "As your mother, I am telling you I love you."

My sobs increased while I rocked with pain.

"Ethel, this is Mama speaking. I love you."

I felt the dam of sorrow breaking up and disintegrating inside me, the first step to wholeness.

❧❧❧

# CHERISHED HEART

Summer's fragrance filled the June air, but my heart felt empty.

Two years had passed since Mother's death. I stood looking out my living room window, thinking about another window and time ... waiting for Daddy.

"Come, Ethel," Mother coaxed. "Daddy's coming soon."

She dressed me in fresh clothes and brushed out my curls. I bounced on the balls of my feet, impatience tugging at me.

"Hurry, Mommy, hurry," I cried before dashing to the chair by the living room window. I hurled myself into it, pressed my 3-year-old nose against the cool pane and waited. This nightly routine lasted until Daddy vanished.

*Lord,* I breathed as a lone tear worked its way from my eye and bathed my dry cheek with its salty warmth. *It's been 43 years since I saw Daddy. If he's still alive, please bring us together.*

Three months later, the phone rang.

"Hello?"

"Hello." Glenda spoke in a flat tone. "A friend of ours met your father in a church in Bloomington, California. He told her he's been looking for you all his life and gave her his address."

"Oh ... oh, praise God!" I cried. I balanced on the balls of my feet, waiting. "Can I have it?"

"Absolutely not." The two words punched into my heart.

"Why not?" I gasped.

# SINK OR SWIM

"Your father was no good. Mother never wanted you to see him — ever — because his family was a mess."

*Click.*

My mind reeled. *God, you heard and answered my heart's cry.* He allowed my father to find a contact person. He'd been looking for me. *Why did Glenda even call me when she had no intention of passing on the address?* My heart sang, then groaned. So close and yet so far.

A month passed. Agony choked me. A friend's father prayed with me. "Call your sister," he instructed. "She'll give the address to you."

My trembling fingers dialed Glenda's number. *Please, please, God,* I prayed. She gave me the address.

That night, I sat down to write to the father I'd loved and missed for more than four decades. I smoothed out the priceless paper containing his address. *Dear Dad...*

Five days later, I held a miracle in my shaking hand — a white oblong miracle in the form of an envelope. I held it against my thudding heart. Forty-three years of searching and longing ended in that moment.

*My darling Ethel,* Daddy wrote. *Praise God I found you. Praise God I found you. Praise God I found you! Your sweet little face has been with me every day since I left.* Floods of tears blurred his next words. *I'm coming to see you in two weeks. Love, Daddy.*

☙ ☙ ☙

My 84-year-old father and his brother stood in the

driveway of my home, along with my son and his family and neighbors, as Eldon and I drove up to the house.

"Oh, dear," I exclaimed, fisting and relaxing my hands. "I can't meet my father in front of all those people. Park in the garage."

I escaped to our bedroom, much the same as I'd done more than 20 years earlier, while Eldon waited at the front door. *What if he doesn't like me? What if I don't like him?* I wrung my hands.

Eldon said, "Are you going to stay in the bedroom all day? Let's go, Ethel."

My heartbeat thumped in my ears as I walked down the hall into the living room. There stood my father, arms open wide to receive me, just like Eldon before him — and Jesus. An eternity passed before I reached him. He wrapped me in his arms, accepting, loving and for all time.

"I've loved you all my life," he choked, nestling his aged cheek against mine. "I never stopped searching for you. Never."

He released his grip to push me to arm's length. "You're so beautiful," he exclaimed as our tears waltzed together.

Daddy stayed a week. Wherever we went, he and I sat in the back seat, he with his father's arm always about me. The years of separation and desolation melted away like butter on a Phoenix sidewalk.

"I remember your face pressed against the window every time I came home from work," Daddy said. He swallowed. "That last day, I had just come home and your mother ordered me from the house, right then, right there. I grabbed your little hands, determined to take you with me. Your mother grabbed your feet suspending you between us.

"Your terrified screams caused me to drop you. I left. The last thing I saw was your face pressed against the window, crying and waving at me." He swiped at a tear. "I have prayed every day since then that God would help me find you."

A year later, Eldon and I renewed our wedding vows in celebration of our 25th anniversary in the presence of our five children, their spouses and our whole church family. Daddy walked his little girl down the aisle. Joy rocked the house as heaven and earth celebrated.

Daddy passed away just before his third planned visit. I continue to praise my God for bringing my daddy back into my life in time.

ॐ ॐ ॐ

"My mother was a good woman," I stated. "She ran a mission for years and brought many people to the Lord. She loved people and was respected and loved in return."

"She wasn't there for you," Ginger, my good friend, repeated. "Jesus said the truth will set you free. And the truth is she was never there for you."

Her words stung.

"You're right," I sobbed. I allowed the painful truth to illuminate my soul, the next step to wholeness. "She repeatedly sent me back to Irene when I begged and begged to stay with her. She never asked why." I daubed at my eyes with a soaked tissue. "She never abused me, but never supported me emotionally, either. Only Glenda was good enough for her total love and attention. I never measured up."

We sat in silence as the Lord began to open my understanding. *You're just like your daddy,* he said. *She couldn't stand anything that reminded her of him or her failure. But, Ethel,* he continued, *I've always loved you.*

Again I stood in our living room. Suddenly I had a vision of a little girl sitting on dark steps. Then I saw her sitting on an angel's lap while Jesus stood nearby.

Jesus turned to look at me and then pointed to the little girl. "That's you," he said. "It's because of me that you are who you are today. Your love and compassion grew out of those times. I was there all the time. I never left you."

The vision vanished. Jesus had let me know who I am and why I am here. His compassion drives me. I never want to see anyone treated as I had been.

### Whole Heart

Eldon and I went to a local hospital to visit a lady in 1990. I felt horrible.

"Could you find a nurse to take my blood pressure?"

His eyes mirrored shock. I never asked for anything. He hurried from the room, returning minutes later with a nurse in tow. She slapped the cuff on, pumped it up and released the valve.

"You're going to the ER, Mrs. Bomley," she said as she removed the cuff. "Right now."

"You have congestive heart failure," the attending physician informed me before staff whisked me off to CCU. He ordered a medication to tame my galloping blood pressure. It plummeted, and I lost consciousness.

I looked up. Jesus relaxed on a regal throne, smiling down at me. "You've been asking to come home for some time, Ethel." He leaned on the chair arm. A warm smile tugged at his mouth. "Do you want to stay here or come to heaven with me?"

My heart skipped. *I can go with you now?* He nodded, but held up a hand to stay my decision, then I saw a vision and watched Eldon and our church family file past, shaking their heads. "No, no, no," each intoned.

I turned back to my Lord. "It looks as though I'm still needed. I guess I'll stay." Jesus flashed a beautiful smile.

"Okay," he said and vanished.

The doctors discovered scarring on my heart.

"When did you have multiple heart attacks?" one asked.

"Thirty years ago, before I reached 22," I answered.

"You're a lucky lady," he responded. "Your mitro valve has been leaking at 50 percent, there is thickening around your heart and your lungs were almost filled with fluid. You had about two days left on the planet." He gave me a pointed look. "Go home and do *nothing* for a year."

# CHERISHED HEART

Eleven months later, Eldon found me sitting, holding my head in my hands. I had just returned from getting our mail.

"Are you okay?"

"No."

This time, the doctor had me flown to Spokane on the verge of a major heart attack. The specialist, Dr. Golden, scheduled me for heart cauterization. Our pastor joined us in prayer, committing the procedure and future to God.

Later that day, Dr. Golden waltzed into my room.

"Mrs. Bomley, I don't know how to tell you this, but you have a perfect, beautiful, normal heart."

Our eyebrows shot up.

"Normal?" we chorused.

"Normal." He grinned.

"What about the scars?" Eldon asked.

"Gone."

"And the thickening?" I added.

"Let me put it this way," he explained. "You have never been as healthy in your whole life as you are at this very moment."

The next day, I returned home to enjoy what I couldn't as a child — hiking, shoveling snow and making my first snow angel at age 54.

఩఩఩

Three years after God gave me a new heart, the abuse of my formative years flooded back, determined to rob me of peace and joy again. *You're not as good as other people*, the enemy lied into my spirit. *You're not as good a minister as others are.*

*Not as good* pumped through me with every heartbeat. *Not as good* clawed at my mind. The lies multiplied until I felt suffocated.

Then I learned that Irene and her sisters had been badly abused themselves as children. Her father beat them and locked them in their basement, as she had done to me.

The Holy Spirit nudged me. I ignored him. He nudged me again, with gentle persistence, like a horse in search of a carrot.

*You and Eldon took classes to help abused people. You've led support groups for abused people. Didn't you learn anything from them?*

"What?" I finally opened my heart to listen.

*What did you learn from those sessions, daughter?*

"The abused become abusers."

Oh. The light of understanding burst in and pierced my spirit. I lifted my hands to God.

"Father, I forgive Irene. Right now. Completely. Forever."

God's love washed over me, sweeping away every terrifying memory like pebbles before a tidal wave. And his grace sought and found all traces of lingering resentment against my mother and dissolved it in love's onslaught.

Total forgiveness toward everyone removed the final barrier to complete wholeness.

# CHERISHED HEART

I moved to our family room. There I spotted a photograph taken when I was a little girl. I picked it up and examined it.

"I was a pretty girl," I said to the little smiling me. Long eyelashes framed bright blue eyes set in a face of flawless skin. Lovely brown hair curled at my shoulders.

"I *was* pretty." I wept with the joy of newfound truth.

I continue to reach out to all the unloved, unwanted people I meet. I hug them. I love on them, telling them they are loved by the one perfect father. I introduce them to my best friend, Jesus. This passion will continue to drive me — until my last day on the planet.

# GUIDING ME HOME
## THE STORY OF ARBY SHOWN
### WRITTEN BY ELLEN R. HALE

Sleep eluded me. I tossed and turned in my bed as familiar, but unwelcome, emotions crept into my mind. Gripped by a combination of hopelessness and anger, I threw off my covers and fled from the room.

*I have to get out of here!*

The cliff rose 100 feet above a canyon less than two miles from my home. Once I shut the front door, I ran through the dark, cool night. My feet pounded the gravel road. Soon, I would leave the road and rush through the field. I would jump from the cliff, I would plunge toward the canyon and I would die on impact.

The sound of a truck engine cut into the thoughts flooding my mind. Slowing to a walk, I saw my father driving toward me. I was standing at the precise point where I planned to leave the main road and navigate through the field.

"Hey, I just wanted to check on you," Dad called.

"I'm fine," I lied.

I escaped the house many times for a midnight run, hoping to relieve the torment in my head. Sometimes I stayed out for hours, noting a porch light passing every half-mile — the only evidence of the real world. Coincidentally, this was one of the few times my dad or mom hunted me down out of concern for their 15-year-old son struggling with bipolar disorder.

I climbed into Dad's truck, and we turned home, the headlights dispelling the blackness surrounding us.

❧ ❧ ❧

Entering my freshman year of high school in 1995, I had no clue who I wanted to be. But I knew who I *didn't* want to be — my older brother, also known as "preacher."

My parents, two brothers, sister and I never missed a church service. I didn't always want to go, but attendance was not negotiable. For whatever reason, my older brother demonstrated his belief in God to our classmates even in elementary school. He prayed before eating lunch, he carried his Bible to classes and he pointed out when kids disobeyed. No one liked "preacher."

Clearwater Valley High School offered me a fresh start. I would not allow kids to pick on me.

"You want to try something?" one of my friends whispered at the homecoming football game.

"Sure," I replied nonchalantly.

I joined a group of guys and left the school property. Stopping by the river, someone pulled out a bag of marijuana and a pipe. As we got high together, I was thrilled to fit in with the crowd.

My friends and I began smoking pot regularly. We enjoyed hunting and getting high. Once, two friends and I hunted grouse. Suddenly, one of the birds flew out of the woods. My buddy spun around and shot, missing the grouse, and blew off my friend's hat instead.

*Wow, that was close.*

We each smoked another joint.

In 1996, severe mood swings started taking over my life. I often felt happy-go-lucky one minute and in the next moment mad at the world. I frequently flew into rages. At night, I dwelled on everything I hated about myself and what I did wrong that day. Running on the roads around my house seemed the only way to release the negative energy consuming me.

A psychiatrist diagnosed me with bipolar disorder and prescribed medication.

I didn't understand his explanation about chemical imbalances in our brains, but I knew I needed help and desperately wanted change. Despite starting treatment, I sometimes considered suicide.

❧ ❧ ❧

The 90-degree heat outside my girlfriend's house matched my boiling anger over the fight we just had. Jumping in my father's Ford Taurus, I cranked up the music and sped away. I envisioned the steep embankment overlooking the river, a perfect launching point.

Now that I had my driver's license, I possessed a new weapon for killing myself. I stepped on the gas, swerving up the winding roads with one destination in mind.

Coming around a corner, I lost control of the car and

landed in a ditch. My head smashed into the windshield. As flames engulfed the car, I pushed open the door. Not far away, a man watering his lawn witnessed the accident and extinguished the fire. He drove me back to Kathleen's house.

Kathleen and I had been church buddies ever since her family moved to the area. We began dating in eighth grade. After our heated argument and my accident, I sensed she would break up with me.

I had no choice but to call my dad, who was on his way out the door at work.

"I wrecked your car," I confessed.

He didn't care about the vehicle.

"Are you okay?" Dad asked.

I couldn't believe it. Dad only cared about *me*. Minutes earlier in the car, I had thought no one cared about whether I lived.

Amazingly, I didn't require medical attention. I cleaned up my face and resigned myself to one reality: I was alive.

⮞⮞⮞

The barrel of the rifle pushed against my chest. This was no Halloween trick. My friend's eyes flickered with dangerous determination.

The six-day trip over Halloween weekend in 1998 had taken a detour from elk hunting in the Montana mountains to drunken escapades.

# GUIDING ME HOME

One night, I chose not to drink while my three buddies got wasted.

"I'm going to drive us off the mountain," I informed the guy who owned the pickup truck we were using.

"No, you're not," he retorted.

"Look, you guys are all drunk, and I haven't been drinking tonight," I explained. "So I'm going to drive."

He shoved his rifle into me.

"Give me my keys," he growled.

I handed them over. As I suspected, he swerved erratically. Flying around one curve, he nearly collided with another truck. The driver jumped out and pointed his hunting rifle at our windows, chewing us out for our careless driving.

The next night, we had consumed all the alcohol in the house where we were staying and decided to leave for a beer run. On the way back, our truck clipped a car at an intersection. Instead of stopping, my buddy accelerated and peeled out. Another vehicle from the scene chased us for 20 minutes before we finally eluded him.

A state patrolman showed up at the house the next morning to write tickets for speeding, driving under the influence, disturbing the peace and committing a hit-and-run accident. The driver had to spend the night in jail, and I miraculously survived the trip without injury or arrest.

But that wasn't the case later in my senior year. Although medication began to control the symptoms of my bipolar disorder, I continued to behave recklessly.

Riding around with some friends in town, I asked

them to drop me off because I wanted to talk to an acquaintance we passed. Drunk, I approached him and realized I didn't know him after all. I sat down on the curb, waiting for my ride to return, when I saw a police officer approaching.

I darted away and hid in the bushes outside a bank.

"Come out with your hands up!" the officer ordered. He pointed his gun at me.

He handcuffed me and took me to the station on suspicion I planned to rob the bank. When the officers realized I was only a drunk kid who meant no harm, they called my parents to pick me up.

&#x1F330;&#x1F330;&#x1F330;

"So, what are you going to do after graduation?" my co-worker at the restaurant asked me as post-high school life loomed.

"I have *no* idea," I admitted.

She knew about my enthusiasm for hunting and the outdoors.

"I have a friend who's an outfitter, and he's always looking for guides," she offered. "If you want, you could check that out."

After talking to the outfitter, I was sold. Three days after graduation, I moved out of my childhood home and headed four hours away to guide big game hunts in the North Fork of Clearwater National Forest.

Living in a remote cabin and working with few days

off, I began to miss Kathleen. We had reunited five months after the car wreck and continued dating. After I began guiding, we saw each other infrequently. But I loved her and didn't want her to get away from me.

That New Year's Eve, I prepared a quiet candlelight dinner for us and asked her to marry me. She said yes even though my job forced us into a long-distance relationship.

Our pastor, Kelly Lineberry, married us on August 25, 2000. After a five-day honeymoon in Coeur d'Alene, I returned to work and didn't see Kathleen for more than two months. Access to phones was spotty, too. I was able to call only once or twice a month. When I visited our home in Culdesac, I brought a stack of letters I had written to my wife as a peace offering.

After two years, the long-distance marriage took its toll on both of us. I was thrilled to secure a few days off one weekend.

"Hey, honey, I'm going to come home this weekend," I told Kathleen over the phone. She worked as a hairstylist at a salon.

"I've already got plans with my friends," she replied coldly. "So don't even bother."

I came home anyway, clearly annoyed with my wife. My friends were hosting a bonfire party in the woods with plenty of booze, and I went without Kathleen. Flirtation between me and one of the girls at the party soon progressed to forbidden kissing.

Even though I was drunk and mad at Kathleen, somehow my conscience kicked in. *I can't do this to her.*

# SINK OR SWIM

Afterward, the knowledge that I had made out with another woman burdened me. I had crossed the line this time and done something I truly regretted. Kathleen could never know what happened, so I determined to improve our marriage.

❧❧❧

For the first five days of the mountain lion hunt, my client and I did not find many tracks. The hunt had been physically demanding as we plowed through waist-deep snow. However, a trapper informed us about tracks he had seen, so we headed to that area. Sure enough, we found the tracks.

The next morning, we discovered no evidence that the mountain lion had left the area. Accompanied by my walker hound, Reno, and redtick hound, Annie, we trudged along in our snowshoes tracking the lion's trail.

Around noon, we located a fresh bed where the lion had been, which boosted my confidence. We spent the cold, overcast January afternoon climbing over two creek drainages. With an hour of daylight left, I realized I needed to leave a marker for my client, who was a mile behind me. At the marker, he knew to follow the trail downstream until reaching the main road in a couple miles. Meanwhile, I focused on rounding up my dogs.

This country was fairly new to me. Snow began falling as darkness set in. I kept hiking through my exhaustion, hoping I was at the correct creek drainage. The sound of

# GUIDING ME HOME

Annie's bark pierced the air. The dogs and I reunited at the bottom of the slope, glad to see the road that would take us back to my truck.

Under the weight of my 30-pound pack, I struggled to move forward through the foot-deep snow.

*Are you ready to come work for me?* I sensed God speaking to me.

I had ignored him for so many years and made so many mistakes, but here he was, trying to get my attention again.

I dropped to my knees in the middle of the road, weeping with a dog in each of my arms.

"Yes, Lord, I'm ready for a change," I cried out. I knew what I must do.

The lights of a truck coming toward us illuminated the night. The outfitter's search for me ended when he found us a half-mile from my truck.

Back at the motel, I thanked the outfitter for helping me.

"But this is the last hunt I'll be guiding. I'm going home."

My guest and I returned to our hunt the next day and finally harvested the mountain lion. Then I turned toward home, to work for the God who saved me.

ॐॐॐ

Kathleen was furious that I quit my job. She was unable to work while she recovered from shoulder surgery. "You did what?" she exclaimed when I called to tell her the news.

"God wants me to come home," I said.

"I don't care what God wants you to do. We have bills to pay!"

Back in Culdesac, I applied for any jobs available. Despite my strong resume and references, no one offered me a position.

When I received my final paycheck from the outfitter, another argument with Kathleen erupted.

"I know we don't go to a church, but we're giving a tithe to a church from this check," I informed her. I wanted to express my obedience to God and my gratitude for his provision in our lives.

"How can you want to give money away when you don't have a job?" Kathleen was livid, but I stuck to my word.

In the three months I looked for work, I started attending church. Just when I had given up on landing employment, the pastor told me his cousin was hiring. He immediately gave me a job cleaning air ducts for furnace systems.

Kathleen had begun attending church with me on occasion, and God put a desire in my heart to minister to the youth. Around my 21st birthday, I received a surprising call from my former pastor, Kelly, about the open youth pastor position at The Life Center. He knew all my faults — exactly what I had done and what I had failed to do. He chose to ask the kid who snuck marijuana into youth camp and drank vodka out of a water bottle at Wednesday night church if he was interested in being a youth pastor. I told Kelly I would pray about it.

"Lord, if this is what you want me to do, I want each board member to say yes. I don't want any argument among the church leaders. If this is your will, let the process go smoothly."

When Kelly called again, I realized God answered my prayer completely.

"There was no argument on the board," he told me. "Everyone said yes to you serving here."

Kathleen, who recognized God at work in the situation, and I quickly found full-time jobs back in Kamiah that allowed us to relocate easily. In just more than half a year, I had transformed from a man guiding others through the wilderness for sport to a servant following God into the unknown future.

☙ ☙ ☙

Five kids attended youth group at The Life Center when we arrived. As God used me and the strong team around me to meet the needs of the youth, the number grew dramatically. On Wednesday nights, we eventually sent out three 12-passenger vans to round up the kids for church. We strived to make each person feel important and loved.

Changes began to happen at home, too. I finally came clean to Kathleen about cheating on her. While she was understandably upset and angry at first, the Lord eventually helped her to forgive me for all my failures during our many years together. No matter what I had done, she had always stood by me. Our joy overflowed when our son, Ridge, was born on February 26, 2004.

That summer, I announced plans for a youth missions trip to Canada. As a fundraiser, we decided to cut and sell firewood.

On the mountain, my father and I worked on the last portion of the 150-foot red fir we felled. The butt of the tree, more than 15 feet long and 3 feet in diameter, was all that remained. *Smack!* The branches of a nearby tree struck me in the face again, interfering with our progress. I started the chainsaw and placed it against the trunk. As the tree toppled, I realized nothing else secured the last heavy log in place on the slope. Dad stood directly below the log.

I screamed as the log knocked him down and rolled over his body, like a rolling pin flattening dough. I shut off the chainsaw and rushed to his side.

A hunter always aims to shoot a bear in the lungs. Once struck, the bear is only able to run about 25 feet before collapsing. The bear's last breath is a deep moan. I had heard that death moan numerous times, and now that same moan came from my father's body. Convinced I approached a dead man, I knew my first aid and CPR training wouldn't work. Instead, I cried out to God.

"Father! Father! I need a miracle right now," I pleaded again and again.

# GUIDING ME HOME

Suddenly, my unconscious dad drew in a huge breath. I called down to the rest of the group to call 911. The helicopter arrived in an hour, though it felt like we were stuck on that hill for days. The chopper landed a half-mile away, so we lifted Dad onto a backboard and carried him to the spot.

There was only room for the pilot, the two medics and the patient. As we loaded him inside, he looked me in the eyes.

"I forgive you," he said. "Make sure you get all the wood."

As the chopper took off, I feared those would be the last words I heard from my dad. Yet I knew he was receiving the best care possible.

*Should I really get the wood? Or should I disobey Dad?*

We were an hour from town, so I decided we should finish our work quickly. We stacked the firewood inside several trailers and headed back.

In my shower, my emotional dam burst. As the water ran down my body, tears of guilt and frustration stung my face.

*God, please don't let him die. He is such a good example of a loving father, and I can't bear to repay him with pain and suffering. His support through the years brought me to this moment of leading the youth group on a missions trip. Please let him live.*

Soon, we sped to the hospital in Lewiston, more than an hour away. When we arrived, we found the doctors preparing to release Dad. He suffered no broken bones, punctures or internal injuries. God had healed him in a powerful way!

In fact, he jumped right back into his job at a lumber mill, though he switched to a less physically demanding position until his aches and bruises disappeared.

A year to the day of the logging accident, the youth group departed for Regina, Saskatchewan. We experienced a great time serving at a church that needed some remodeling done and ministering to the needy in the city's homeless shelters. The trip wouldn't have been possible without both my earthly father and my heavenly father.

❧❧❧

A hunting trip in the North Fork marked my 25th birthday. While my friend and I were there, I developed a sore on my body. I consulted a doctor once I returned. He suggested exploratory surgery, but I wasn't interested. My regular physician diagnosed me with a staph infection and prescribed an antibiotic.

Two months and many sores later, I felt extremely weak. Kathleen's doctor had returned from an educational event where she learned about methicillin-resistant *Staphylococcus aureus*, or MRSA, a strain of staph resistant to most antibiotics. MRSA can be fatal.

"No wonder you're not doing well," said the doctor. "The antibiotic you've been taking won't work for MRSA."

By this time, the infection had spread to my lungs and

turned into pneumonia. I called my boss at my full-time job and told him I was too sick to work.

My condition worsened. I struggled to leave the house even for short trips. If I drove three minutes away to rent a movie, I needed to sleep before I regained the energy to actually watch the movie. Daily tasks like eating and going to the bathroom required amazing effort.

One Sunday morning, I lay on the couch while my family was at church. A John Wayne movie played on the TV. *I'm going to die. It's coming. I need to accept it.*

Through sullen eyes, I saw my dad come in the door.

"What are you doing here?" I asked.

"I came to pray for you."

"But you have church this morning. Why are you missing church?" I couldn't comprehend his actions. I never saw my father miss church once. I wondered why he didn't wait until after church to come.

"I'm going to pray for you."

Kneeling on the floor beside me, he placed his hands on my head and my chest. He prayed fervently, like I had never heard him pray before. Once again, my father demonstrated that he valued my life more than anything else. With him and the Lord fighting for me, I knew no person or illness would ever prevail against me.

From that morning on, I began to feel better. But four months passed before I was well enough to return to work.

☙ ☙ ☙

# SINK OR SWIM

After six years as youth pastor, I found myself lacking vision and direction for the ministry. An emptiness filled my heart. During the last 60 days of 2008, I fasted and prayed for God to reveal what he wanted me to do next. No answer came.

My pastor, Kelly, announced to the church that we would kick off 2009 with 21 days of fasting. Even though I didn't want to participate, I chose to join my church's fast and continue seeking a response from the Lord. Finally, I felt him leading me to take on the position of associate pastor.

*How can that be, Lord? Kelly's mother is our associate pastor.*

My confirmation came in February when she resigned the position. God's timing was perfect, and I began my new duties in June. I love working with our ushers and greeters to make visitors feel welcome at The Life Center and meeting with guests to assimilate them into the church. I oversee our life group ministry, which consists of small groups of members meeting together during the week. And I strive to promote the church in the community, always making Jesus Christ look good.

The Life Center has changed since the years I attended as a child. The church no longer focuses inward, but focuses outward. We are no longer self-serving, but community-serving because we believe that's what God desires. When Kathleen and I returned in 2003, we were among the youngest people attending. But through reaching out to the community and showing them how

# GUIDING ME HOME

The Life Center is "making life better" for everyone, the congregation has grown.

I now recall that when I was 14, a church member prophesied that I would be a leader for Christ. I ignored that promise from God for many years, but since the night he confronted me on a snow-covered road in the mountains, I have responded to his call. *Yes, Lord, I will work for you.*

꙰꙰꙰

Answering the phone, I heard the quavering voice of a young woman full of despair, prepared to end her life. I invited her to find refuge at our house and talk to Kathleen and me.

She had been in our youth group, confessing at age 18 that she had been raped from the time she was 12. The perpetrator had threatened to kill her and her family if she told anyone. She finally had, and we supported her in court as he was prosecuted.

In her moments of crisis when she was suicidal, I knew how she felt. At our home, we read the Bible, prayed and talked until we knew she wouldn't harm herself.

"I understand where you are. I have felt the way you feel." My words overflowed with compassion. "Please turn to God and trust in him because he's the only one who can pull you through these emotions."

I remembered the way my dad stopped me at the crossroads near our home as a teenager. God used my parents numerous times to guide me onto the path toward him. Now I prayed the Lord would use me as this troubled girl's guide toward life and salvation.

# CONCLUSION

*Sink or swim?* We say swim. We are throwing you a life ring and reaching out to you with the stories in this book.

As I read these stories, my heart was filled with joy and my eyes were filled with tears. These are my kind of people. These are God's kind of people! Imperfect, damaged people who are finding a better life. They have not arrived, but they are on an amazing journey.

A long time ago, religious people were upset with Jesus because he hung out with tax collectors and sinners. Jesus responded by giving them a piece of medical information that translates well in describing the true heart of God: "They who are well don't need a physician, but those who are sick."

We at The Life Center understand life is hard and people are wounded. The motto on our sign is "Making Life Better." It is not just a saying, it is what we believe. It is our experience with creator God. He really loves us. He really forgives and cleanses us. He really heals and accepts us.

Historically, we know this because Jesus came to earth showing us the heart of God when he healed broken hearts and set people free from their past. Jesus died on a cross and rose from the dead to rescue us. For some people, things that happened a few thousand years ago don't mean a lot when they are battling the dangerous and troubled waters in their own lives. For them, the real-life stories in this book shout out hope. Shouting out the fact that God's love can rescue them and they can be saved.

The people in this book made a move toward God. They said a prayer. They returned to a church that would love them and help them. They had some relapses. They said more prayers. They found some good friends.

It is your move now. You can say some prayers, return to a good church and find some new friends who really care about you, too. You are just the kind of person God is looking for. You are the kind of person we are looking for at The Life Center, too. Come on in, the water is great!

*Pastor Kelly Lineberry*

# We would love for you to join us at
# The Life Center!

We meet Sunday mornings at 10:10 a.m. at
4432 Highway 12, Kamiah, Idaho 83536.

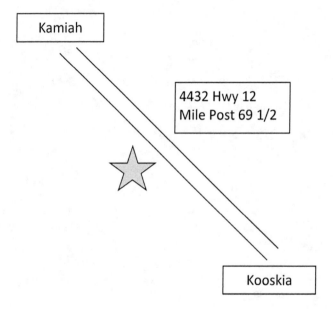

Please call us at 208.935.0362 for directions.
Visit our Web site at www.thelifecenterpcg.org,
or contact us by e-mail at thelifecenterpcg@gmail.com.

For more information on reaching your city with
stories from your church, please contact
Good Catch Publishing at
www.goodcatchpublishing.com

# GOOD CATCH
# PUBLISHING

Did one of these stories touch you?
Has God used this book to impact your life?
If so, we want to know!
If you have testimonies or prayer requests,
please leave a comment on our blog at
www.goodcatchpublishing.blogspot.com,
or write to us at
Good Catch Publishing
4074 NW 169th Avenue
Beaverton, OR 97006

We'd love to be praying for you!